GUIDE
TO
HUNTING
DOGS

© ATP – Chamalières – France – 1998

© 1999 for the English edition:
Könemann Verlagsgesellschaft mbH
Bonner Str. 126, D–50968 Cologne

Translation from French: Jadwiga Billewicz and Dick Nowell
Adaptation and editing: Josephine Curtis and Naomi Laredo
Typesetting: SMALL PRINT, Cambridge, England

Project Coordination: Bettina Kaufmann and Nadja Bremse
Production Manager: Detlev Schaper
Assistants: Nicola Leurs and Alexandra Kiesling
Printing and binding: Mateu Cromo, Madrid

Printed in Spain

ISBN: 3-8290-1730-8

10 9 8 7 6 5 4 3 2 1

GUIDE
TO
HUNTING
DOGS

Claude ROSSIGNOL
Alexandra CACCIVIO

KÖNEMANN

CONTENTS

The adult hunting dog 44

Breeds of hunting dogs 64

The hunter's companion

The origins of the hunting dog

The hunting dog is without doubt the oldest friend and helper of the human race. A friendship as old as the hills, that has deepened with the ages.

It was probably some time between the Old Stone Age and the New – that is, getting on for 15,000 years ago – that dogs and hunters began to team up. The earliest bones found near human skeletons at Neolithic sites belonged to the species named *Canis familiaris putjani* by Linnaeus, the eighteenth-century Swedish naturalist.

European origins

Then there was *Canis familiaris palustris,* the 'dog of the peat bogs,' found throughout what is now Northern Europe. Little by little this primitive dog spread over much of the globe, starting with Russia, Asia, the Middle East, Britain and Southern Europe. From there the dog was introduced to North Africa, while another branch of the family arrived in Egypt from the east. At the dawn of recorded history there appeared *Canis familiaris intermedius*, probably a cross between the peat bog animal and the wolf. This species had the makings of a breed.

Almost six thousand years of selection

Pictures of hunting dogs from prehistoric times are rare, but they were inextricably bound up with the emergence of civilization itself. As early as 4000 BC, dogs were being used for hunting in Egypt, Mesopotamia, the Sahara and Eastern Europe. No one who is familiar with ancient Celtic culture can doubt that the hound was an honored figure there. One of the more unexpected results of the Crusades was the enrichment of Europe's breeds of dog, and at around the same time the first specialist breeds began to be used in falconry. These were the ancestors of the modern pointing dog. The hunting packs of European kings and nobles were very highly regarded throughout the Middle Ages, and at their close it was the English who emerged in the sixteenth century as the foremost scientific breeders. It was in England also that the first international dog show was held, in 1859. This marked the beginning of an international system of breed standards and registration that is now worldwide.

The Gray Dog of Saint Louis IX of France, one of the first reputed purebred dogs, was brought back to Europe by this king after a spell of captivity during a Crusade. He had been impressed by its powers of pursuit, and it remained a favorite of European kings. It is one of the main ancestors of the griffon nivernais.

The dog: general features

The breed standard gives a minutely detailed description of the dog's appearance. Experts use this to assess a dog's looks, but it also enables us to deduce some of the qualities that the animal will show in the field.

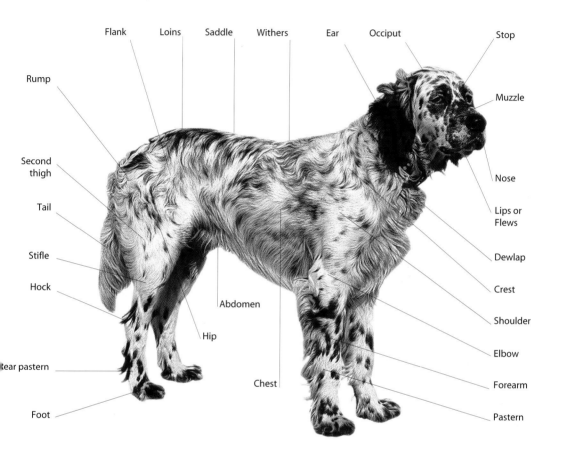

A dog's appearance is specified for each breed in an agreed standard. The way each breed should look is described by dividing the body into clearly defined areas. The use of key terms, such as the 'stop,' the 'point of the shoulder' or the 'withers,' enables the characteristics required of any particular breed to be defined with precision.

The body of a hunter

When choosing a dog it is easy to be sidetracked by its looks, and to neglect the qualities which will make it a useful hunter. This is only natural, but good looks and style are just a bonus.

Practically speaking, the shape and build of a working dog have a direct bearing on what it can do. For example, stamina – the dog's capacity to make a sustained effort without becoming too tired –

certainly depends on individual temperament and energy, but it is also a function of the dog's build. And without stamina, a dog can hardly bring its talents to bear in practice. Besides, what is worse than the disappointment of seeing your dog give up the chase when others are in full hue and cry? How a dog is put together is of great importance, because limbs and joints are the mechanism of this living machine; and a good back and firm loins are what give a dog its speed and distance.

Where the line of the back is fairly short and slightly curved, the dog will be able to gather its legs underneath more easily and gallop faster. A less well-formed dog always weakens and tires too soon. So the best choice is a well-built dog, one that will make a companion you can be proud to own for many seasons to come.

9

Buying a puppy

Where to buy your puppy

*Buying a puppy needs a good deal of thought: this little bundle of fur
is going to be your companion for at least ten years.
How should you set about it?*

There are a great many ways to go about finding your ideal partner, but for hunting dogs there is one golden rule: go to a user if you can. Find someone who hunts. Of course you can get a good deal at a pet store that has a litter from a hunting breed for sale. But in this situation it can be difficult or impossible to check quality of the sire and dam – unless of course the storekeeper can show you a star-studded pedigree from your national Kennel Club.

The time-honored place to look, and still one of the best, is the small ads. Hunting magazines, for instance, are full of offers, and with a little patience and caution you have every chance of making a good buy. There will also be a range of prices, so any buyer can choose a puppy to suit their pocket. More and more private advertisements are appearing in free newspapers everywhere. Here again, if you take the trouble to go and see a number of advertisers, it should not be too hard to flush out a good dog at a reasonable price. Of course, you need to be a little more wary, or you could be disappointed. There are also small ads to be found on the Internet. Whichever route you take, it's always best to see the puppy in its original surroundings, preferably with its mother, and get an idea of the breeder's skill and care.

It's worth going to a real specialist

If you have set your heart on a particular breed, the breed society or your local dog society will be able to give advice. You can get their contact details from your national Kennel Club (see page 61), and they will have a list of breeders of pedigree dogs and their addresses. Or you can consult the national Kennel Club itself, which should keep a file of all the litters that have recently been registered.

It pays in any case to buy a puppy with a genuine pedigree from an established breeder, even if it costs a little more. Many trainers of hunting dogs raise litters of several breeds, and they have the advantage of being available to give advice when you need it. That can prove to be a really valuable after-sales service.

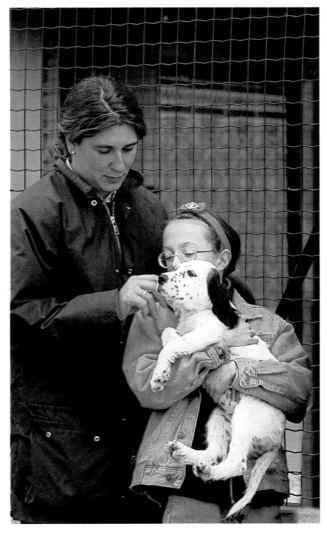

If you're buying a puppy as a present for the hunter in the family, it's best to go to a professional, who can help you make the right choice.

Choosing a breed

Deciding on a breed is not easy. Physical appearance is an important factor: you are, after all, going to live with each other day in, day out. But there are also many other practical considerations.

There are currently almost two hundred breeds of hunting dog recognized by the International Canine Federation (ICF), not counting sighthounds. That means a couple of hundred reasons for finding it hard to make up your mind. Most hunters keep more than one kind of dog in the course of their hunting life. Your choice will usually depend on your circumstances, including family circumstances. The opinion of your hunting friends will probably influence you, too.

Make an informed choice
Of course, if you are a complete beginner, you have to find out what you can for yourself. The traditional method is to buy a couple of books, which may or may not give the full facts, and may even be reprints whose advice is past its sell-by date. You read articles about the various breeds in dog magazines, and maybe go to a dog show to get your prejudices confirmed. You fall in love with one dog's good looks, and go to a breeder who, of course, will sing the praises of this particular breed. Of course it's the best! The breeder offers you a puppy that is bound to make you the happiest dog owner in the world. Or so you fondly believe. But a different, more rational approach might help you to avoid disappointment.

Choose a dog for your intended purpose
Most domestic dogs have been bred for the climate

and landscape of their region of origin, as well as for the job their owners wanted them to do. Hunting dogs are no exception. Every breed has been selected for a particular purpose, and that means that each is a specialist in a particular terrain or a particular type of game. So, though it is dangerous to generalize, pointing dogs are recommended for fowl and hounds for other game. Retrievers and other dogs that bring in a kill are multi-skilled dogs that can be used for all sorts of small game, and sometimes even for larger quarry. Lastly, terriers and dachshunds can also be all-round hunters, though they do have a preference for furred game and dry land.

Ask the breeders who hunt
But all this is just theory. What really counts is the dog's line of descent, its family. The least risky procedure is always to buy a rabbiting dog from a hunter of rabbits, a dog for woodcock from a shooter of woodcock, and so forth. This is better than going through lists of the supposed aptitudes of each breed. You should also check that your future partner's trainer goes in for the same kind of hunting as you are planning yourself. This is important, because the breeder's selection will have been made with a particular aim in view, and a quality that is appropriate to one style of hunting could be a handicap in another.

For hunting small game, bassets are a good choice, like these large blue Gasconys, excellent at flushing rabbits out of thickets.

The cocker spaniel, like all retrievers, is an asset in almost every kind of hunt.

Choose a breed to suit the territory

In choosing a breed you also need to consider the kind of terrain you will be hunting over. Small breeds do best in gorse or scrub and on heath or moorland, while the larger ones are suited to meadows, marshes, coppices and woodland that is clear of undergrowth. In mountains and hilly country, heavy breeds find that their weight tires them: climbing is hard work, and so is braking on the way down. A small dog will do a good job, and there is a lot to be said for one that takes up less room and can be carried around easily in the car. After all, that is how we go hunting nowadays. There is such a variety of breeds that you are sure to find one that really fits.

If you have a disappointment or two, don't give up. Bear in mind that all pedigree dogs possess the characteristic talents and aptitudes of their breed, even though they may not necessarily win first prize in the standard beauty competition.

Dogs that point, especially the pointer itself, are experts when it comes to wildfowl, and unbeatable in open country.

Taking care of the paperwork

Whether you buy from a professional breeder, an amateur or a friend, it's always wise to put things in writing. And the formalities of identifying and registering your new puppy are your responsibility.

When you buy a puppy, the golden rule is to make a written agreement and get it signed. A sales contract should spell out the return policy and should include a guarantee against genetic faults and health problems. If the dog is sold as purebred, this should be indicated, and the seller will normally provide the pedigree and registration papers.

Licensing
Wherever you live, you must have a valid license for your dog or dogs, which generally needs to be renewed every year. In the USA, licenses are issued by your local city or county government, and in most places you have to show a current rabies vaccination certificate. If you move, you may have to get a new license – almost certainly if you move out of state.

Identification
In the USA, dogs must wear their license tags at all times, as a means of identification. In the UK, dogs have to wear a collar carrying details of their owner and home address. There is no legal requirement for permanent identifying marks on a dog, but owners wishing to safeguard their dogs can opt for permanent identification.

Tattooing is the conventional method. Dogs are usually tattooed on the ear. It is not a painful procedure and takes only a few minutes. The unique number tattooed on the animal is entered in a national register. A microchip is the modern option. A tiny electronic chip carrying a unique code is inserted under the dog's skin. The chip can be read with a scanner to identify the dog.

INTERNATIONAL CERTIFICATE OF VACCINATION

CERTIFICAT INTERNATIONAL DE VACCINATION

INTERNATIONALER IMPFPASS

for DOGS ● pour CHIENS ● für HUNDE

Your dog's vaccination record is like a passport. It must be shown if you want to take the dog abroad, or if you leave it in boarding kennels. Some countries make exceptions to their quarantine regulations for dogs with valid vaccination certificates, though the UK still doesn't do so at the time of writing.

Registering your purebred puppy
For a puppy born in the United States to be registered by the American Kennel Club (AKC), the sire and dam must already be registered. A litter is collectively registered with the AKC by the owner of the dam, who is considered to own the litter. The AKC sends a 'litter kit,' including individual registration forms for each puppy. On selling a puppy, the breeder must certify the date of sale and the name of the buyer, otherwise the puppy can't be registered.

A breeder will usually give the new owner the dog's pedigree and registration papers. The only exception is when the breeder considers that the

Whatever the legal health requirements where you live, you owe it to your puppy to vaccinate it against common canine diseases – and to keep the boosters up to date.

puppy is not up to show standard and unfit to be bred from. In this case, the sale must be accompanied by a written agreement, signed by both buyer and seller, stating why the documents were withheld.

In Canada, completed litter registration application forms have to be submitted by the breeder under the Animal Pedigree Act. The Canadian Kennel Club then sends an individual application form for each puppy, containing a transfer of ownership section where the name and address of the buyer must be entered. Dogs have to be identified by a tattoo or microchip before the new owner takes possession. A non-breeding agreement must be signed before leaving with a new puppy, but this can be neutralized if the puppy grows into a dog of acceptable breeding quality.

In the UK, the owner of a dam which has produced a litter of pedigree puppies must register the litter with the Kennel Club. Both the sire and the dam must already be registered, and the owner has to produce the dam's pedigree and proof of the paternity of the litter from the sire's owner. In some circumstances, the owner may require the registration to be endorsed; for example, so that any young born to the puppies cannot be registered (if they are not to be bred from), or so that an export pedigree cannot be issued (if the owner doesn't wish to have the puppies sent abroad). When the Kennel Club is satisfied with the details, a Kennel Club Breeder Registration Certificate is issued for each puppy, with a change of ownership registration form on the back. When the puppy is sold, this certificate is given to the new owner.

Microchipping

This is the modern alternative to tattooing. An electronic chip, about the size of a grain of rice, is inserted under the dog's skin with a hypodermic syringe, just like an injection. The chip is usually placed between the shoulder blades or at the neck. This is harmless and, like a tattoo, it lasts a lifetime. The microchip can be read with a scanner, and animal shelters and rescue centers are equipped with scanners to check all strays brought to them. The owners can then be traced via a national database of microchip codes.

Choosing a puppy

It's vital to choose the right puppy. People all too often rely on looks, but a good choice takes an individual dog's character into account as well.

When you are presented with a fine litter, deciding which puppy to take is really tricky. In the first few days of life there really are very few signs to go by. You may pick a lively puppy, or prefer one sex or the other. You may like a particular color, though of course the tricolors' coats, especially those with a saddle, start out just black and white in any case. Right from the start, though, a kinked or off-center tail will be noticeable, as well as some deformities of the jaw indicating an undershot or overshot bite. But a proper selection can't really be made until after weaning. So curb your impatience, and don't make a hasty decision: the ideal time to make a considered choice is when the puppies are from three to six months old.

Go for a well-formed dog

One of the primary considerations is the dog's build. Good physical shape is essential in any hunting dog if it is to be really useful. This is not a matter of conforming to some standard, but of basic features common to all breeds. Its stance and paws give an early indication of how well the dog will move. Remember that the joints are the machinery of these future athletes, so the mobility of the limbs needs careful inspection. Similarly, a well-proportioned bone structure or topline is a promising sign, which you can often confirm by checking the build of the parents. On the other hand, some features are still hard to judge. The color and texture of the coat may change, and the dog's final height can really only be guessed by comparison with the rest of the litter.

Remember that hunting is the object

After studying the physical characteristics, you still need to consider the important question of behavior. How does the dog react both to normal circumstances and to specific events? Within a litter, an order of precedence starts to emerge in the very first days,

Only after weaning do the characteristics that are going to turn a puppy into a useful hunting partner start to show.

Making a choice from a young litter is hard. At first, you really only have the sex and color to go by.

but it doesn't become established until the thirteenth week. Only then can the young hunter's character begin to be assessed. The expert Konrad Lorenz said that animal behavior is a succession of reactions to particular circumstances which result in a given action. There is no need to go into technical details, just to appreciate that the puppy's behavior is determined by various internal and external factors. An 'urge' is a predisposition to carry out some instinctive activity, such as tracking. 'Motivation' is the dog's readiness to carry out a particular task, and the 'stimulus' is a change in its surroundings, sensed by the dog, that pulls the trigger.

Selective breeding of hunting dogs has adapted their sense organs to certain situations, producing the characteristic behavior and aptitudes that a breed shows in action. This is what we call the breed's 'inbred hunting style.'

Love at first sight – for both of you

When you are picking a puppy from a litter with a particular aim – hunting – in view, pay special attention to its character. You can quite quickly and easily gauge the puppy's reaction to your presence. If it slinks off when you bend down, this is a sign of timidity, which could cause problems later. A puppy that stays in its corner and shows not the slightest interest in your visit may well remain an independent-minded dog all its life, which is just as undesirable.

But if a puppy comes up to you, that is a good sign of friendliness. Where puppies and adult dogs are kenneled together, go for the one that always tries to make contact with its elders and adopts the submissive posture (lying on its back or side) that indicates a well-balanced individual.

A healthy puppy is a good bet

The puppy's state of health is another important factor. You can tell by its general appearance how healthy it is: look for a shining coat and a confident, lively, inquisitive look. The belly should not be a great ball. Puppies should always have a good appetite: they shouldn't be picky or slow eaters, wandering around at feeding time.

Lastly, be sure to ask the breeder for the vaccination record, so as not to miss the boosters. It would be a shame to let all your care in choosing a puppy go to waste by neglecting this simple precaution.

Living together

First contact, transportation and housing

So you're off to fetch your new pet!
There are many changes you will have to face.

Once the purchase has been completed, it's time to go home. This will certainly be your new companion's first car journey, so give it some thought. If you can, bring a helper along (a child is fine, so long as they are over 10) to look after the puppy on the way back. Better still, have someone drive you, or at least drive home. That way you can do the looking-after yourself, and reassure the puppy. Even so, it is best to provide a traveling box. Whatever you do, and whatever kind of vehicle you have, the puppy must go in the back, never scramble over to the front.

When the puppy arrives at its future home, it's the first few moments that really count. They may even have a lifelong influence. It's important to avoid any kind of trauma if at all possible. The start of a puppy's life with a new owner should represent a completely natural weaning process. Don't spoil your puppy by making too much fuss: this will tend to prolong its dependency, just when a little independence is called for.

Be gentle but firm

The new arrival should find a place ready for it, and the limits on your puppy's actions must quickly be made clear. A kennel does make for fewer problems, but if your pet is to live in the house you really mustn't be soft when it comes to jumping up on the bed or sofa. There can be no babies' privileges if you want 'no' to mean anything later on. But you needn't be too severe, just firm. Instead of wallowing in delight, keep your eyes open for the first few days, while your puppy is settling down with a new home and new friends. You'll have to keep on your toes at first, but it gets easier once the puppy finds out what's what. And your attentiveness now will be well rewarded by good work and loyal service when you go hunting. The best trick of all is simply to use the puppy's name really often, with plenty of eye contact and a pat. That's the way for a puppy to learn that you care.

It's always a great occasion when a new puppy arrives, but it's best to be well prepared.

Your first visit to the vet

The vet is a dog's 'family doctor.' Your vet will be able to take better care of your puppy's health if you introduce them to each other early on.

A responsible breeder will always have a new litter examined by a vet to ensure that all the puppies are in good health, but you should still take your new puppy to the vet for a thorough medical examination.

A thorough check-up

The vet will take your dog's temperature and check its pulse and reflexes. He or she will make sure that the animal isn't suffering from any infections and will examine it for malformations. For example, the tail should not be kinked or offset, and the bite should be neither overshot nor undershot. The vet will check your puppy's gums to make sure that the teeth are coming through properly. The eyes and eyelids (especially the third eyelid, absent in humans) must also be examined. All these factors can affect future health and wellbeing.

If your dog's breed is subject to certain conditions, the vet will check for signs of these. Hip dysplasia, for example, is quite a common joint disease in larger breeds and leads eventually to arthritis. Progressive retinal atrophy (PRA) is a hereditary disease that results in deteriorating vision, cataracts and sometimes blindness.

Worming and immunization

The vet will check for external parasites and may also examine your puppy's stools for internal parasites. Treatment will be recommended if necessary. Young dogs should in any case be wormed regularly.

Finally, the vet will recommend an immunization program for your dog. A typical schedule is shown opposite, but the vaccinations needed depend on the breed and on the diseases prevalent in your area. Legal requirements also vary from place to place: for example, rabies vaccination is compulsory in most states of the USA but is not required in the UK.

A small traveling box will make for fewer problems on your puppy's first visit to the vet.

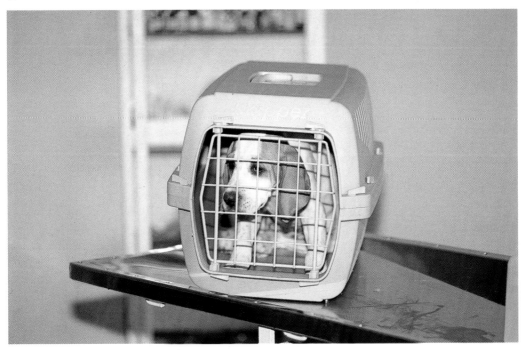

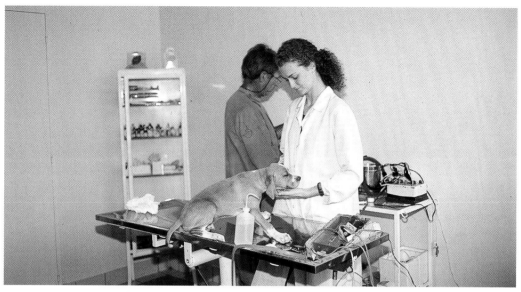

Regular health checks are essential to give your future hunting partner a good start in life.

Typical vaccination schedule

First and second vaccinations for puppies under a year old

Around 8 weeks	Canine parvovirus Infectious canine hepatitis (Rubarth's Disease) Tracheobronchitis (Kennel Cough) Canine distemper (Hardpad)
Around 12 weeks	Canine parvovirus Infectious canine hepatitis (Rubarth's Disease) Tracheobronchitis (Kennel Cough) Canine distemper (Hardpad) Leptospirosis Rabies
Around 5 months	Borreliosis (Lyme Disease)

Boosters

Every 6 months (in high-risk areas)	Leptospirosis
Annually	Rabies Leptospirosis Borreliosis (Lyme Disease) Tracheobronchitis (Kennel Cough)
Annually or every two years	Canine parvovirus Canine distemper (Hardpad) Infectious canine hepatitis (Rubarth's Disease)

Descriptions of diseases protected against

Canine parvovirus	A highly contagious disease attacking the small intestine and sometimes the heart
Infectious canine hepatitis	A highly infectious disease caused by a canine adenovirus and affecting the liver, kidneys and eyes
Tracheobronchitis	An infectious disease causing inflammation of the windpipe and bronchial tubes
Canine distemper	An airborne viral disease spreading through the bloodstream and nervous system
Leptospirosis	A bacterial disease often carried by rodents and spreading through the bloodstream
Rabies	A viral disease of the nervous system spread by wildlife, causing personality changes, convulsions and paralysis
Borreliosis	Caused by various organisms transmitted by ticks and leading to swollen joints and fever

Feeding throughout growth

Feeding a puppy properly means providing the right sort of food and the right amount of it. This is crucial to the puppy's future development, and any mistake now could have serious consequences.

When you buy a puppy, remember to ask the breeder how he or she has been feeding it. Professional breeders should provide a diet sheet and usually a sample of food to get you started. Of course, you can change your new puppy's food later, to suit your preferences or even your budget; but you must do this gradually, staging the change over a number of weeks. Puppies should always be given food that is both appetizing and easy to digest. They need more than an adult of the same weight: more protein and minerals and a higher energy value. Because they don't yet have all their adult teeth, don't feed them chunks that are too big or too hard. In the early stages a suitable meal might consist of (unsweetened) evaporated milk, chopped meat, and rice or bread. The simplest course, though, is to buy commercial puppy food.

Commercial foods cost a little more, but are still good value
There are canned puppy foods on the market that provide the extra energy, protein and minerals puppies need. Alternatives are biscuits for soaking and dried foods for rehydrating. Dry food is much more convenient to prepare, and you can supplement it with powdered puppy milk substitute, reconstituted with water at about 39°C/100°F in the proportions recommended by the vet or manufacturer. It's better to avoid cow's milk and ordinary powdered milk, because their constituents are not properly balanced for puppies (unless you add an egg yolk in the old-fashioned way). Later on, if you want to prepare your own feed, you could give a mixture of about 50% cooked rice, 30% lean red meat, 15% vegetables, and 5% of a vitamin supplement. If the meat is rather fatty, use 45% meat, 25% rice, 25% vegetables and 5% vitamin supplement. The proportion of fatty meat needs to be higher to meet the puppy's protein requirements, and because the fat has a higher energy content, the amount of rice must be cut to keep the diet balanced.

Good feeding and exercise: recipe for a champion
The daily ration for a puppy is one of the hardest things to work out, although commercial foods do carry a guide according to the dog's weight. It is simplest not to limit the amount, but to leave the bowl down for no more than a quarter of an hour at each feed. Whatever kind of food you choose, puppies need three meals a day until they are six months old, and two a day up to one year. For larger breeds you can continue to give two meals a day up to

For reasons of hygiene, puppies' meals should be prepared immediately before being given, and any leftovers cleared away fifteen minutes later.

In the first months of life, playing provides enough physical exercise for a puppy's development.

eighteen months, or even longer if necessary. By spreading the food intake over the day, you avoid digestive upsets or, worse still, twisted stomachs, which can result from eating too much at one sitting. Throughout the growing period, take care not to give your puppy scraps at family mealtimes. If you do, the dog will quickly get into the habit of begging, a fault that is extremely hard to correct later. Along with proper feeding, your future hunting companion needs the right sort of exercise. Up to six months, just playing is enough to allow the puppy's physique to develop while it lets off steam. After that, you should start going for regular walks. Between

If puppies are fed biscuits, they must also be given milk. Only soaked biscuits should be given to very young puppies.

six months and one year, a fifteen- to twenty-minute walk five or six times a week is ideal, and the puppy's first training sessions will complement this exercise. A few months before the start of the first hunting season, you can reduce the frequency of your walks: just go out every other day, but stay out for thirty or forty minutes, so that the dog's constitution gets used to more sustained effort.

Don't forget about fresh water

Good feeding is vital, but remember that living things consist mostly of water, so you must provide drinking water in addition to the liquid in the feed. Puppies need a constant supply of clean water. Put a clean drinking bowl in a suitable cool spot and refill it with fresh water several times throughout the day.

Rearing your puppy

Good basic schooling is clearly crucial.
If this is tackled right, it can even provide
an introduction to more formal training.

To some extent, rearing a puppy means teaching it good manners. First and foremost, however, it involves setting up lines of communication between two creatures: it's a breaking-in process. This is useful in itself, but it will also form the basis of successful training later on. Dominating the dog's will is not what is needed: more a kind of understanding, resting on a few simple ground rules.

Get to know your dog

If you want a loyal companion and, later, an effective partner, you must first observe and understand your puppy's character. Every individual differs in temperament; and the bonds you forge now will determine the course of your whole lifetime partnership.

The first rule your dog has to learn is obedience to authority. Indeed, it is part of dogs' nature to need a master: kind and affectionate, but a master none the less. There must be absolutely no doubt who is in charge. Always keep calm, and avoid any display of bad temper or disappointment when your dog fails to understand.

It's important to teach your puppy the difference between the sound of its name and a summons. The puppy must learn that when you say its name this is not a command to 'come,' but just a signal that it is being addressed. The simplest method is to say the puppy's name now and then in the course of a conversation that is mainly about something else. That way, the dog learns to pay attention without bounding over every time it hears itself mentioned.

Be fair and consistent

Bad habits are generally hard to correct, while a little care can often prevent them getting a hold in the first place. So try to anticipate tricky situations and don't give your dog the opportunity to make a mistake.

It's only natural for a puppy to take an interest in anything and everything. But if the slippers are in the cupboard, then they won't be in temptation's way. And there is no danger of your puppy chewing a feeding-bowl that is cleared away after every meal.

The daily walk is a specially good

The first bonds that are formed between puppy and owner often set the pattern
for their lifelong relationship.

Out on a walk, especially just after a meal, is when the puppy will learn to relieve itself away from home.

between your order and a specific action. Use only short, simple and meaningful words. Above all, learn to recognize when your pupil is really making an effort. Even if what the puppy does is not quite right, a little reward – a pat, or maybe just a kind word – will encourage it to persevere. The other fundamental principle, of course, is that the dog must know what 'no' means. It's quickly learned, and useful on many occasions. But schooling is not all about restriction. Your pupil has to learn 'go!' as well. In short, education based on obedience and good behavior is what suits a dog's nature and future role as a hunter.

Toilet training

Toilet training a puppy calls for patience. Only by going out often will you get the puppy to understand that it is supposed to relieve itself outside. It makes things easier, though, if you remember that the crucial time is usually straight after waking and after meals. Time your walks accordingly.

On the very day your puppy arrives, it's a good idea to go straight to the place you have chosen as the 'toilet,' before letting it go into the house. Then keep a watchful eye for a while. When the characteristic behavior appears – sniffing the ground, turning around and starting to squat – just carry the puppy to the 'toilet' and be ready with congratulations as soon as it has relieved itself.

teaching opportunity. Walking on a lead gets a puppy used to acting in partnership with its owner. The natural submissive instinct is triggered, which is a useful first step. No longer at liberty, the puppy starts to behave better and gets used to contact with its handler. The time will come when mutual empathy will make all the difference to a good day's hunting.

Let the puppy set the pace

Take care not to go too fast, and allow your puppy time to mature. Teaching a puppy – or a child, for that matter – means adapting to the pupil's age and capabilities. Never be afraid to go over the same lesson again and again, until it clicks and the puppy makes the association

A walk is the ideal time for teaching a puppy, and it is often out walking that the first hunting experience occurs.

Organizing your daily routine

In many cases a hunting dog is also the family pet. That calls for a fair amount of organization, especially when the family goes away for the weekend or on holiday.

Hounds, traditionally housed in a kennel and yard, are rarely concerned when their owner goes away.

For as long as the dog has been mankind's partner in the hunt, which means millions of years, the two have also been sharing their daily lives. But though in the past they may have had the same lodgings, civilization has brought great changes in the relationship between humans and their animal companions: what was natural once would not do at all today. The rules by which we live have changed and are still changing, and dogs' place in human society has to be constantly redefined.

Doing without your dog

The ideal arrangement is to have a small kennel or at least a basement or garage where your dog can spend the night and part of the day, while the adults are working and the children are at school. But there are times – family weekends away and of course holidays – when the daily routine has to be broken. You

cannot take your dog everywhere all the time. When on occasion the dog must come along, do not let the experience turn into a nightmare – for either of you. You should never leave it in the car while you go to the restaurant, for instance. If you really can't avoid leaving the dog for a short time, and even if you have a good traveling box, make sure that the car is in shade and leave a window open. Remember, too, that what is in shade now may not be by the time you come back.

If you decide to take your dog on holiday with you, do be sure to check beforehand that the place where you are going really welcomes dogs.

Someone to look after the dog?

If you are going away for more than a weekend, the most sensible thing is probably to board the dog with someone else. Don't assume that this is bound to be traumatic; remember that, whether your dog comes with you or stays behind, life is going to be different for a while from the rest of the year. If a relative, a neighbor or a friend can look after it, that is the simplest solution, and the least expensive. If you can, choose someone the dog knows well – a good hunting friend, perhaps. The only danger then is that this person may try so hard to win your dog's affection that they set up a few bad habits in the process. Don't let this bother you: everything should go back to normal with a return to familiar circumstances.

If your pet normally eats dry or canned dogfood, your deputy will have an easier job of it: you only need to lay in enough provisions for there to be no need of a change of diet. On the other hand, if your dog is used to your own home prepared mixture, it might be better to organize a gradual changeover to dry food during the month preceding your departure. Biscuits are much easier to feed, and cleaner too.

Today there are more and more boarding kennels, an excellent solution for holidays if they are properly equipped and run.

Boarding kennels: a little more expensive, a lot less worry

Leaving your dog at a properly run boarding kennels is by far the best course. Of course, you must do your research beforehand, just as you would for your own holiday destination. You can ask at the vet's, ask friends, or just go back to the breeder where your dog came from. They may be one of the many breeder/trainers who also run boarding kennels. Wherever you choose, visit the kennels and check the facilities. You need to feel confident that your choice is best for all concerned. Otherwise you will worry, and your dog will surely pick up your stress. It's a good idea to take the dog there a few days before you yourself leave, so that you can check that all is well and set off without worries. Remember that dogs are social animals, so while you may make new friends on holiday, maybe your dog will also enjoy the company of other dogs.

If you pick a commercial kennels where they also do training, this is an ideal chance to improve your dog's hunting skills. A holiday course never hurt anyone. Get a fixed agreement on fees beforehand, though, preferably in writing.

A holiday in the country, staying in a holiday cottage or with relatives, gives you an opportunity to get away with your companion without too many problems.

Training a hunting dog

Basic principles of training

You can't make a dog ready for the field by improvising a training schedule as you go along. Sound basic training is necessary to bring out its innate qualities.

You can profit from a young puppy's trust in you to teach it a great deal with relative ease. On the other hand you must never, ever, betray your puppy's trust. That is the first golden rule. Be scrupulously fair throughout training and keep your individual roles well defined. To err is human – and also canine – so don't reprimand your puppy without reason. The first step is to get the puppy to do things that are more or less instinctive. To achieve this, you need to use commands combined with reward or punishment, as appropriate.

There are three ways to give commands. When the pupil is close by, voice and hand signals can be used – or a whistle, in the case of gundogs. When the dog is at a distance from the handler, as with hounds and terriers, you can use a horn. Voice and hand signals are all you need initially, certainly until you move on to hunting-related lessons. The tone of your voice must always match your gestures, to help the puppy understand. Body language governs dogs' behavior amongst themselves and they are very sensitive to it. When addressing your future hunting partner, clear commands are good ones. For the message to be clearly understood, it must be as short as possible, and always use the same words so that they become a kind of code.

Rewarding your dog

Reward generally takes the form of a tidbit accompanied by a friendly pat and a few kind words. A chunk of dry cheese or a bit of biscuit is ideal. You can also use a few chocolate drops or a sugar lump, but be careful not to spoil a puppy or it won't stay keen for a reward. If your pupil earns several treats in a row, break off the lesson and return to it later. And don't forget to let the puppy see the tidbit before beginning work, otherwise it loses its value as a reward.

Don't traumatize your dog

The use of physical punishment is a controversial issue. In the first place, it can only be appropriate when a dog refuses to perform a task it has fully understood. Never use it in other circumstances. It is never, ever, a way of making the dog understand you.

Dogs are not 'broken in,' they are educated. At all events, physical punishment must be immediate, brief and moderate. A severe reprimand or withdrawal of privilege are equally effective with a sensitive dog. But do think about the side-effects of any form

A reward, in this case a chunk of cheese, is the best way to motivate your puppy during training.

Obedience is the basis of all training.

of punishment: shutting your dog in its kennel as punishment could turn the kennel into a prison, something to be avoided at all costs.

Obedience

The training of a dog hinges entirely on its obedience to its handler. From the day you take charge of your new puppy, you should be building up this type of relationship. Like every individual growing up and developing in a civilized environment, the puppy will gradually learn where the limits are. When a dog lives with its owner, as the gundog breeds are often privileged to do, there is no shortage of teaching opportunities and the puppy will learn that much faster. If your dog lives in a kennel or has its own place outside the house, you have to take advantage of every outing, every walk and every mealtime to establish who is the master. Because that's what it is all about. Either you have to be the pack leader or the dog will, with disastrous consequences.

Graduating to working life

The puppy's basic schooling is followed by its first experiences of encountering game in natural surroundings. If you have access to open countryside and can introduce your dog to wild game, it is much more stimulating. If not, wait for the start of the hunting season rather than rushing things. Don't confuse the job of a professional trainer, who has to work all year round and is subject to deadlines, with the satisfaction of training your own dog. This can often be done at a more leisurely pace which is enjoyable for both dog and handler. We are always too impatient. Hunting is a natural instinct and can develop more or less spontaneously. There is no need for anxiety: your dog's true abilities will show through only when conditions are

Pros and cons of the electric collar

This product of modern technology is illegal in the UK but is increasingly widely available. Although regularly used by professional trainers, it is not recommended to the inexperienced amateur. It requires expert handling and a full understanding of canine psychology. Clumsy use of the electric collar can have a devastating effect on some dogs. On the other hand, in the hands of an experienced trainer it can solve specific problems, such as teaching recalcitrant gundogs not to chase game and training hounds to follow only the desired quarry.

right. And don't forget that a youngster has not yet fully developed all its faculties and that some individuals take longer to mature than others.

The whistle can take the place of verbal commands as training progresses.

The key words

If you want a dog to obey you, it is essential to make yourself clearly understood. To make this easier, base your training on a few key words.

The best recipe for success if you are training your own puppy is always to express yourself simply and, above all, clearly. Successful training depends on good communication between pupil and trainer. Never lose sight of the fact that dogs only understand words they have been taught: launching into a tirade peppered with insults is utterly pointless and ridiculous, if not disastrous. You will only succeed in bewildering your dog and, in any case, all the puppy will remember from your fit of temper is your body language.

Clear-cut commands

Inevitably, even before placing your pupil in a situation where it can show its mettle in the field, you will need to use commands to make the dog understand the limits on its actions. The easiest way to achieve this is to teach a command which means that something is, quite simply, forbidden. 'No' seems to be the obvious choice. If your puppy lives with you, there will be no shortage of opportunities to show your disapproval and the command will be assimilated very quickly. If you want to speed up the learning process a little, use 'no' to teach the puppy to leave a tidbit alone, only taking it when the command 'take it' is given. This unequivocal command will avert tricky situations in the future when the dog comes across a species it must not chase, such as small birds.

Fine-tuning your commands

Once the 'no' is well established, it is good practice to modify it with 'steady,' a command which urges restraint on the dog. You can do this by taking advantage of any instants when the dog hesitates, wondering how to behave. 'Stea-ea-dy,' said in a forceful manner, will prompt it to be careful and well-behaved. For example, if your dog is about to do something stupid, 'steady' will act as a reminder that it has already learned through 'no' that it would be well advised not to pursue that particular action. Again, if the dog's delight at your arrival is too boisterous, 'steady' – possibly followed by 'sit' – will bring it back to its senses. Later, 'steady' will prove very useful in the field, particularly for checking any desire to give chase, and even for steadying the point.

The puppy must learn early on to leave game alone. One of the applications of 'no' is to encourage restraint when face-to-face with a bird.

'Sit' and 'down'

Young hunting dogs should save all their enthusiasm for seeking out game. In all other situations, they should display self-control and drop on command.

Since a dog must never be left to its own devices in the field, you should take steps to ensure that you are always in control. The only way to achieve this is by teaching your dog to stop instantly on hearing the appropriate command, so you must teach it to sit or to lie down. In dog-training parlance this is called dropping on command. Both positions can be very useful. There are several ways to teach your dog to sit. The most effective is to lift the dog's head by placing a hand under the chin and at the same time to give the command 'sit.' You can also press down on the dog's hindquarters, but this tends to make a stubborn dog stiffen up instead of sitting.

An unequivocal command
The word 'down' has become universally accepted as the peremptory command to lie down and above all keep still. Though its practical use when hunting is perhaps limited, it is a more or less essential discipline and is certainly the most effective way of keeping a dog under control at all times. The value of this command is therefore above all educational. To appreciate its force, think of the 'down' as a kind of fuse that enables you to halt any action instantly.

When given the command to sit, the dog should remain still and wait for a new command before moving from this position.

The 'down' is the sign of an obedient dog: the pupil's head should be kept flat on the ground.

Putting the emphasis on control
If your dog moves from the 'sit' or the 'down,' placing a hand on its head and repeating the command several times will encourage it to stay put. Then you can gradually begin to back away, raising a hand and repeating the word at regular intervals. After a few sessions the hand signal should be enough. If the dog disobeys, you must take it back to the precise spot it moved from and begin again. If you think your dog has worked well, you can forestall any confusion by returning to the dog in order to reward it. After a few lessons you can begin giving the commands from a distance. Finally, if you want to replace the verbal command by a whistle, you should blow the whistle first and then shout.

Walking on the lead

*Putting a lead on a puppy is an excellent way
of socializing it, which will reap rewards
in the field.*

When you are teaching a puppy to walk on the lead, never fall into the trap of engaging in a trial of strength and forcing the dog to give in and follow you. It is much better to use less traumatizing methods, so that the lesson takes place in a calm and friendly atmosphere. A good way to begin is by simply making the puppy wear a collar round its neck. Easy, just put it on. This may appear insignificant but it is an important step in itself, though easy to achieve.

Introduction to the lead
A good ploy is to attach a rope about a yard long – in effect a lead – to the collar and to let it trail. In this way the puppy becomes used to being restricted but, because it still has freedom of movement, accepts the rope more easily than if you were holding on to it. When you first start working on the lead, it is best to keep it short. This prevents the puppy from lunging forward to the end of the line. It also helps the puppy to feel the slightest movement of the handler's arm, teaching it to obey and making the rest of its schooling easier.

Lessons in compliance
Most puppies get upset when you first ask them to walk on the lead. You can get over this problem by making frequent changes of direction. This

*Short but frequent walks are the best
form of schooling.*

focuses the puppy's attention on where you might be heading next and takes its mind off the lead. A few minutes' walk every day, and the dog will soon understand that the collar and lead are signs of an outing and will be delighted to see you pick them up. Teach the puppy to walk at your side by making it walk behind you to start with. Then allow it to come alongside. The puppy is used to being held back and will look up at you inquiringly. A friendly pat from you, and the dog will stay at your side.

*A long cord attached to the
collar gives a good start in learning
to walk on the lead.*

Questing

Questing is the way a dog seeks out game.
The dogs that are best at finding game are the ones that know
how to quest properly.

A dog can be taught to find game by learning a procedure well within the scope of most hunting dogs: quartering. When you get to the training field, sit your dog beside you 'upwind,' i.e. facing the wind. Remove the lead and have the dog sit quietly at your side for 30 seconds to a minute. Then 'cast' or send it to the right or the left, encouraging it with a command of 'hi on' or 'hi seek.' Clap your hands and run alongside for a few strides. After letting the dog quest out for twenty or thirty yards, call it back with two blasts on the whistle while you head in the opposite direction. The dog, raising its head at the sound of the whistle, sees its handler disappearing and also changes direction.

Giving encouragement

The moment the dog draws level with you, encourage it to continue questing by raising your arm and calling 'hi on' again. When the dog has gone the same distance as before, repeat the command, this time signaling in the opposite direction. You must make a very definite half-turn at the beginning of each loop, almost as if you were making the loop yourself, so that the dog passes close to you on its

As the dog quarters, direct it by raising your arm and shouting encouragement when it passes you.

return and is not tempted to head off into the wind. Do the same when you call it back to change direction; if you open up the angle by running forward about ten paces, your dog will be led naturally into the right response. This pattern of loops made by the dog is no academic exercise: it maximizes the thoroughness and effectiveness of the quest.

Retaining a passion for hunting

However, making perfect 'figures of eight' is not enough if the dog is to point game or its scent. It must also be questing for the scent of the game. The dog's nose and intelligence must remain on alert and it must step aside from its course if necessary to 'study' any smell. Enterprising dogs seem to be on the increase nowadays, and this is a valuable attribute. Speed and range in the quest never stand in the way of a satisfactory result – in fact, quite the reverse is true. While eagerness in a dog is easy to control, you can't teach initiative. You must look to extending the range of the quest before trying to regulate it. When your dog can perform 'figures of eight' with the regularity of a metronome, reduce their size gradually by giving a few blasts on the whistle.

Give plenty of encouragement when you 'cast,' to increase the dog's eagerness in the quest.

Pointing

Among breeds classed as 'pointing' dogs, this is a natural quality and cannot be taught. But the instinct can be refined through training.

Pointing is the motionless stance with which a dog responds to the presence of game. Puppies start to show this behavior at widely differing ages, and these variations need to be interpreted with care. For example, you can trigger

It's a good sign when a young puppy points a bird, or even a falling leaf that startles it. But despite this instinctive behavior, it may be some time before the dog learns to point game correctly.

pointing in some puppies at three months or even younger, with a bird wing fastened to a fishing rod. Others start to point naturally between five and seven months, some much later still. But this does not mean that if a dog doesn't point at a year old it never will. It could simply be too immature or not have been exposed to the right conditions.

Holding the point
From the beginning, pointing should not be confused with firmness at the point. Pointing will anyway be triggered spontaneously sooner or later, so all the trainer needs to do is put the dog in a situation where it is likely to occur. Firmness at the point can also develop naturally, but not in every case, and this

often requires some work. Holding the point is what makes a pointing dog useful in the field, so it is an essential skill. Only when this is well ingrained can you begin training your dog to 'make out' the point. This means allowing it to walk beside you as you move forward slowly to flush the game. 'Backing,' where a dog freezes when it sees another dog on point, is also indispensable for working as a brace or a group.

Reinforcement
To sum up, training a pointing dog consists of making it grasp the need to remain motionless, at least until game rises. The usual method is to take advantage of the way the dog stands still for a moment on scenting game. As it pauses, slip a lead round its neck to hold it back. You then prevent the dog from rushing in to flush by patting and praising it. When, after successful training, you kill for the first time on your dog's point, go and pick up the fallen game. Don't allow the dog to do it. Retrieving is a separate and equally important skill.

Almost every breed points game in its own way, but in general the British dogs, setters and pointers, are more rigid on point than the breeds of mainland Europe.

Getting your dog used to gunfire

You must accustom your future hunting dog to the sound of gunfire as early as possible. But take great care, or you could make matters worse.

Having an older dog's example to follow helps a young dog to get used to the sound of gunfire. You can use a small caliber weapon or, preferably, a bird scarer to provide its first experience of explosions.

Gun-shyness is a relatively common problem and one that is difficult to overcome. Occasionally it seems to be due to inbred timidity, but in most cases it is caused by mistakes on the part of the handler. The worst thing you can do is fail to train your dog to tolerate gunfire. If your puppy is being trained to replace an older animal, allow the youngster to profit from the seasoned dog's experience. Working together gives dogs more confidence, especially if they are young and nervous.

Avoid big explosions
If you are lucky enough to own the mother of the litter or the puppy you are rearing, you can arrange a lesson as early as three to eight weeks. When they are that young and can copy their mother's behavior, puppies quickly get used to the sound and smell of gunpowder. The easiest method is to let off some small fireworks or a small caliber rifle in a familiar place, such as the kennel or garden, where the puppy feels quite safe. Never take the puppy by surprise, even if it reacts well to this test.

Progress slowly
During training, the dog's natural eagerness on encountering game is often used to help it understand what guns are for and to familiarize it with the sound they make. This is fine, but it is better to accustom the puppy to gunshots that are unconnected with its own work. You might have to shoot game your dog did not wind, and you are rarely in the field alone, so it may hear other shots being fired.
However, nothing is gained by rushing this training. You absolutely must not set off more and more explosions, fire a rifle suddenly, or take your puppy to a clay pigeon shoot in the hope of getting a quicker result. What matters is that the dog does eventually learn to tolerate the sound of gunfire.

Steadiness to flushed game

Good behavior when game is flushed is not an essential hunting skill, but it makes things easier for the guns and is the sign of a well-trained dog.

You don't want to dampen your dog's enthusiasm – only to make it understand that it must not chase game, so take it slowly and gently. If you have access to wild game birds, the usual way of teaching steadiness to feathered game is to use a long check-cord or rope. But don't check your dog too severely when it sets off after a rising bird. A dog that is fearful of being punished might take to ignoring the presence of game. The dog is well aware that the check-cord will prevent it from bounding forward, so just steady it with your voice.

Moderate your dog's exuberance

If you are using farmed birds for training, you can often leave the dog at liberty. Just go up to it at the appropriate point, take your dog by the collar and say a few friendly, reassuring words to calm it. Then make the bird fly off, keeping hold of the dog as it quite happily watches the bird go. Make your dog stay beside you, 'off duty,' for a moment before allowing it to begin questing again. A few short sessions, repeated regularly, are usually enough to quiet the dog's initial exuberance.

Never allow a chase

Any tendency to chase animals, as a predator chases its prey, must be curbed.

A good trick for teaching steadiness to fur is to train your dog not to chase cats.

Slipping the lead back on while the dog is on point teaches it to remain steady when a bird takes wing.

From the practical point of view, a dog that leaps after a bolting rabbit or hare makes shooting difficult, even if it has pointed first. Steadiness to furred game is taught in much the same way as steadiness to birds taking wing. Young dogs give chase most often when game rises from under their nose.

You will find it much easier if you have practiced the 'down,' but this command may not be enough if the dog has formed a habit of chasing. The difficulty is greatest if you hunt in flat open country, where a dog can pursue its quarry by sight over long distances. So the first rule is never to allow a chase. If it does happen accidentally, punish the dog at the beginning of the run if possible, but never when it returns. If you own a cat or, better still, if there are a lot of cats in your neighborhood, teaching your dog not to chase them is a good way to start and is always effective.

Retrieving

*For many hunters, a gundog that does not retrieve
falls short of their ideal of the all-round,
practical hunting partner.*

The retrieve comes second only to the point on the hunter's list of priorities. Besides being a useful skill, the retrieve gives added pleasure to the hunter, and to the dog that finds and brings back the game its owner has shot. Some breeds, especially the old breeds of mainland Europe, are 'natural' retrievers. But, although you can take advantage of this instinct, you cannot always rely on it. A hedge, fence or stream may prevent a dog from marking where game has fallen, or can form a barrier the dog is unwilling to cross. There are also dogs that simply refuse to retrieve certain types of game.

A sharp retrieve

For a dog to be really useful in the field, it must be able to retrieve without jibbing when asked, and to refrain from retrieving when not required. The retrieve on command consists of a sequence of three actions, each in response to a separate, precise order: 'hold it,' 'fetch it,' and 'give.' The most difficult part is teaching a dog to take hold of any object on command. To teach the command 'hold it,' all you usually need to do is give a few tidbits and make your dog wait for the words before being allowed to eat them. Then continue the lesson using a wooden dumbbell. If the dog hangs back, give a tidbit and the dumbbell by turns, in rapid succession, until it gets the idea. Now accustom the dog to taking anything in its mouth, but especially warm animals, such as a freshly shot pigeon or a dead rabbit. The dog must learn to do this perfectly reliably and without hesitation.

The magic words 'fetch it'

The second stage is getting your dog to pick up the dumbbell from the ground. You can only do this very gradually, by placing the object further and further away. The day the dog willingly picks up the dumbbell and holds it until you say 'give,' you've done it! Once your dog will go one step to pick up the dumbbell, it will go ten yards, then twenty. All you have to do now is to walk the dog on the lead, carrying the dumbbell in its mouth, while you repeat 'fetch it' every three or four paces. Those two words tell a trained dog exactly what it has to do. And dogs retrieve all the more enthusiastically if they have difficulty locating the fallen game.

A wooden dumbbell is still the traditional aid for teaching a dog to retrieve.

You won't bring out the natural retrieve in an inexperienced dog by using compulsion.

Obedience

Whatever your dog's breed, obedience to your orders is absolutely essential.

By putting the feeding troughs outside the kennel, you can continue your dogs' training in the open without taking too many risks.

From a strictly practical point of view, it's obvious that obedient dogs make the best workers. Although there are no hard and fast rules, scenthounds, terriers and dachshunds can be trained to obey by repeating an exercise regularly and often, until it becomes a kind of habit. This is a gradual process requiring patience and perseverance. You cannot use force in the field, so this is not the solution. In any case, you want your dog to use its initiative, which is incompatible with over-submissiveness.

A good start in the kennel

A pack must have a certain level of training, and starting with a few lessons in the kennel saves precious hunting time later. The most popular way of training hounds is by doing obedience work at feeding time. This consists of making the pack stay closely grouped in a corner of the kennel while you put the food in the troughs. When the food is ready, make the hounds wait for a signal before allowing them to eat. It helps to have an assistant, at least for the first few sessions, but this procedure takes up only a few minutes a day and produces amazing results very quickly. By moving the trough away little by little, you can even make the hounds walk together in an orderly manner – a sure sign of authority demonstrated by the whippers-in of hunt packs.

You must be absolutely meticulous in your choice of language: it is essential always to use the same words and to keep your commands short.

Use every opportunity

Take advantage of every available opportunity for practical training. Walks are the traditional way of promoting a good relationship between dog and owner. Make use of hunting excursions too, but do not ask too much, especially at first. It is easier to wait until the hunt is over, and then make the hounds walk behind you for part of the way back. A good piece of equipment for this is the couple. You can buy them quite easily, but they are also simple to make, using a choke-chain and two trigger hooks. Every little step forward will give you great pleasure.

The recall

An important aspect of obedience is training your dogs to return to you on command.

When on the scent of game, hounds, terriers and dachshunds will of course tend to leave the hunter way behind. They may get several miles ahead, so it is essential that they respond to being called back. Except in unusually difficult circumstances, a good recall means that you should never have to go home without your dogs, something to avoid at all costs. If you have only one or two dogs, living at home and used for hunting small game, you are unlikely to have problems so long as they are trained in general obedience. A small game animal pursued by one or two dogs is unlikely to travel very far. Standard training techniques, combining the assertion of your authority with patting and giving treats, should suffice.

Sound basic training for the pack
Things get more complicated when you own a pack. For one thing, the fact that the dogs are kenneled means you can't easily develop the special bond that dogs

A horn is used to recall hounds from the pursuit.

living in the home enjoy. For another, the pursuit of larger or faster game takes the pack further away from the hunter. A hunting horn must be used for the recall instead of your voice, and this requires thorough training. Amateur trainers usually lack both sound preparation and the will to finish the job. Dogs aren't generally aware of having completed a task: they will only come on recall out of habit, ingrained by repeating the command until it has the desired effect.

Practice in the kennel
The best time to teach hounds to respond to the sound of the horn is at mealtimes, because their eagerness at the arrival of food makes them pay attention. As soon as they are familiar with the horn, start practicing in natural surroundings. You can back away from them or crouch down while alternately calling their names and giving a few blasts on the horn. When hunting, the recall is often an order to break off the pursuit, so it is sensible to associate the sound of the horn with the command 'stop.' You can work on this when giving food or when entering the kennel, but always when the hounds are doing something positive.

Hound puppies are as obedient to their handler's calls as any puppy. But this natural 'recall' needs to be reinforced.

Giving tongue

*Giving tongue for the first time is an important rite of passage
into the working life of a young dog.*

Reasonably enough, a puppy's owner is always impatient to see it in pursuit of game. For a dog to follow a scent trail while giving tongue is instinctive behavior that will emerge by itself, sooner or later, depending on the breed and maturity of the individual. If you just wait patiently for your dog to mature, it will begin to give tongue. But you can smooth the way: you can trigger the moment when you and the dog become efficient hunting partners. It is most usual, and most effective, to let a puppy give tongue between the ages of six and ten months.

Leave the puppies to themselves

In the past, puppies were left to run free outside the house or farm buildings. They pursued everything that came by and so learned to love the chase. Any puppy that was heard giving tongue was kenneled before it became too independent or picked up too many bad habits. Nowadays, with rare exceptions, we have to use other methods. More or less the only legal procedure is to put your puppies in a paddock and leave them to babble together. By letting instinct take its course, you very quickly find out which puppies are the brightest. And because the puppies don't have to make a physical effort to keep up with their elders, they can learn at their own pace. With this method, they will grasp quickly and easily that their job is to put their nose to the ground and sniff out a track.

A dog that has given tongue is a useful dog

This procedure allows young hounds give tongue at an age when they are their most alert, without making them risk straining their immature bodies. You will have very little time to devote to them when out hunting, and in this way they make useful members of the pack as soon as they join it. What species of game triggers them to give voice for the first time makes no difference to their future hunting ability. Keen hound puppies chase anything they come across, so there is no point in trying to plan for this. The day a dog gives tongue on coming across a warm scent, it has passed the point of no return. It is unhelpful to replicate the experience, in case the puppy develops a taste for that particular scent: you may have plans to hunt something else. When young hounds have given tongue, they can be left in the kennel for a few months until it is time for them to join the pack.

Puppies are best left to give tongue among themselves. This way they discover the pleasures of hunting at their own pace.

Scent discrimination

Teaching scent discrimination takes high priority nowadays, with the need to manage individual species and to combine pleasure with profit.

Dogs that naturally follow only one type of scent do exist, but they are so rare that it is unwise to rely on this untrained instinct. Better to adopt an appropriate program of training in scent discrimination. This means training a dog to hunt only the game you want, and to ignore the scent of other wild animals completely. It is often no more difficult than house-training a puppy, but don't be fooled into thinking that it can be done overnight. The technique is fairly simple and is based on teaching 'right' and 'wrong.'

stopping your dogs following the wrong scent, the more likely they are to learn quickly. The fact that a scent is unfamiliar doesn't stop them following it. For the lesson to be effective, you must stop them only when you are certain they are wrong. And they must very quickly get a chance to spring the game they are supposed to hunt, so that they grasp the difference. If you only hunt where there are few chances of springing the right animal, and where you know you will have to restrain the dogs often, you could dampen their enthusiasm for the hunt.

Teaching dogs scent discrimination has become a necessity, so that hunting quotas can be observed and game species managed individually.

Excellence founded on experience

Scent discrimination doesn't mean that one pack cannot hunt a variety of game. What matters is that it should stay on the scent you put it on. The aim is simply to get your dogs to quest and pursue only the quarry you want to hunt, without being sidetracked by anything else. There are no short-cuts or magic tricks in training: only experience and repetition condition dogs into adopting the appropriate behavior. Patience and determination are needed, as well as skill. Above all, you must be able to tell which animal the dogs are pursuing, sometimes without even seeing it. Use your own discrimination and try never to mislead your dogs. If in doubt, it is better to let them make a mistake than to stop them when they are right, at least at first. But when you are sure the dogs are wrong, never let them get away with it.

Learning in the field
You might think that areas with a wealth of animal species should be avoided. On the contrary, this is exactly where you should take your dogs to teach them scent discrimination. You don't learn to swim by standing on the bank of a river. The more opportunities you have of

The adult
hunting dog

Should your dog live in the house or in a kennel?

There is no reason why a hunting dog shouldn't live in the house with its owner, even in town. But 'to each his own place' is the best ground rule for peaceful coexistence.

It isn't easy to decide whether your dog should live in the house, like any other family pet, or in a kennel. There are no hard and fast rules: every hunter–dog partnership is different. But, however much you love your dog, it is worth remembering that accepting it into the family is not without drawbacks. Even if having your faithful hunting companion at your side gives you great pleasure, you must consider the dog too: try to 'think in dog' to avoid misunderstandings. A dog that lives with the family can certainly adapt admirably to its dual roles of hunting dog and pet. But, unlike other pet dogs, it must maintain its sporting instincts and skills. Wherever you live, the practical problems of sharing your family's everyday life with a hunting dog are no greater than those of keeping any other kind of dog. Hunting dogs are sensitive animals and, given the chance, will become deeply attached to their owners. Sometimes they will even spend the day in your favorite place in the house, waiting for you to come home. Your dog must have a place to sleep in, a kind of 'home' of its own, where it can go whenever it wants. This can be a wicker basket, a plastic dog-bed or just a wooden box.

Dog food, not human food

Living in the house does not usually have any ill effects on the dog's behavior out hunting. If anything, it likely to be more flexible and eager to help. An unsuitable diet is the only real risk. Dogs are frequently given scraps of bread dipped in gravy during family meals, or allowed to eat the leftovers. This means that they are actually getting two or three meals a day, not counting the children's snacks and candy. Avoid this at all costs. An adult dog should be fed only once a day, preferably in the evening, so that it can digest its food at leisure while sleeping. Its diet should be dogfood, balanced and formulated to meet an animal's needs and tastes, not human food. Dogs may enjoy the scent of a hare, but they have no business with the stew! You must control your hunting dog's diet strictly if you want to keep it on top form.

The secret of a harmonious relationship lies in establishing firm ground rules. A dog must have a place of its own to go to, either of its own free will or when sent, and where it can sleep. Constant contact with people is not a good thing. Unless you keep your eye on it twenty-

Dogs that live in a kennel lead more regular lives and often work harder to please their owner.

Dogs that live in the house become companions for the whole family.

four hours a day, a dog will inevitably pick up bad habits which could affect its behavior out hunting. Even an adult dog should only be petted for a reason, which may be simply as a reward for being good. On the other hand, you should devote regular time to your dog, and take it for a walk two or three times a week.

Time together is special

If you live in a house with a garage, a wash-house, a yard or a garden, the dog can spend part of the day inside with you or the family, and the rest of the time outside or in an outbuilding.

Ideally, you should give it a small kennel where it can happily sleep at night or nap during the day. But you must avoid chaining up your dog: it will be much happier loose, even with only a few square yards to run around in, and it is always better to build a small kennel run. If you live in an apartment block, you will have to take the dog out several times a day so that it can relieve itself. You cannot just leave a litter-tray the way you can with a cat. If the whole family is out from morning to night, you must make an arrangement with the janitor or a willing neighbor to take your dog out during the day.

A dog quickly learns why it is being taken out and will only need a few minutes to do its business. Take the dog out with you whenever you can: to collect the children from school, for example, or to fetch the groceries. Frequent walks with a bit of variety are better than hours spent lying about on the couch. The more fun your dog has in your company, even when you aren't hunting together, the more efficient it will be as a hunting partner. But, except when you are working or having fun together, the dog should stay in its kennel. It might not be learning anything useful there, but at least it isn't picking up bad habits to spoil its hunting performance.

Housing the hunting dog

Housing your hunting partner can be a source of worry. From the simplest dog kennel in a small yard to facilities for the professional, there is something to suit every taste and every pocket.

Your dog's kennel is first and foremost its 'home,' not a place where it is shut in. The kennel's main function is to make life more pleasant for the dog ... and its owner. Whether it is newly built or made by adapting existing buildings, every aspect of a kennel must be designed with hygiene and a degree of comfort in mind. But don't forget that comfort doesn't necessarily mean the same to a dog as to a human. It is a mistake to overdo it. Any building you are adapting as a kennel needs to be high enough to contain quite a large volume of air. It must also be well lit, well ventilated because of the smell, but free from drafts, which are dangerous to a dog's health. A building that faces east or south-east is best for housing animals. Choose a sunny spot,

so that the dog can lie in the sun, sheltered from the prevailing winds. The size of building required is proportional to the number of occupants and their size. A hut 8 to 10 meters/10 to 12 yards square should be big enough for one or two dogs. A large run is not essential, as a hunting dog in any case needs to be exercised outside its kennel as often as possible – at least once a day.

Facilities anyone can provide

The plastic-covered square mesh fencing seen on industrial sites can be used to create a fenced yard against an existing building or to enclose a kennel run. It is fairly attractive and easy to put up. Most builders' merchants and do-it-yourself stores stock the panels, posts and fixings you need, in an extensive range of sizes and mesh types. But make sure you choose fencing that is strong enough and high enough for the job. Think about the size of the panels, too, because you have

You must get planning permission before building a traditional brick kennel.

A kennel is 'home' to the dogs. The best way to make them happy there is to pay them a visit from time to time.

make the lower part of the enclosure of galvanized sheets to shelter your dog from bad weather, or install swiveling dish-holders so that you can feed it without going into the kennel. Some kennel kits include flooring. They may have roofing that is soundproofed against the noise of rain, and even shutters for protection against extreme weather.

Barred panels are safer for medium-sized or large dogs like many hunting dogs. An angry dog can break a tooth on square mesh, though this is rare. Some dogs will try to escape, and if the kennel or yard has no roof they can climb up square mesh and get out.

The ideal spacing for the bars is 5 cm/2 in, if you are likely to have a puppy, as it won't be able to get its head through. But bars 8 cm/3 in apart are less expensive.

to get them home. Check the cost of delivery if you can't transport them yourself – you may find that an apparent bargain is not such a good deal after all. Some stores have kennels in their range of garden sheds, but they are often of poor quality for the price. A kennel must be solidly built, and it is worth making a long-term investment in something specifically designed to house dogs. The chances are you will be raising a puppy at some point, possibly to replace an aging companion, and the 'little devil' will be very rough on your beautiful kennel.

Consult an expert

Self-assembly units for kennels have been flooding onto the market in recent years. They used to be available only to professionals but are now mass-produced and within the reach of all. Their greatest advantage is that they can be easily moved. If you rent your home, you will probably hesitate to build a permanent kennel. With these units the problem does not arise: it only takes a few turns of a spanner to put them together or take them apart. You can assemble them yourself, to create a cubicle under a lean-to, a yard against an existing building, or even a free-standing kennel. You can have units made to measure, at extra cost, in order to add a fence to the top of an existing wall or make use of a previously useless corner. And using made-to-measure units opens up many other possibilities. You could

A small, manageable kennel run is always preferable to a large paddock, which can quickly begin to look like a zoo.

*Ideally, your run should face east or south-east, so that your dogs
can enjoy the sunshine, while remaining sheltered
from wind and rain.*

Think about the daily chores

For ease of maintenance, it is best to concrete the floor of the kennel, or give it a waterproof coating. A very smooth coating, though, will be slippery when wet or when there is a frost. Tiled floors should be avoided. Ensure good drainage by sloping the floor at a sufficient gradient toward a drain channel. Or make it slope in every direction toward a drain-hole, with a trap and grill to catch solid waste that could block the drains. The floor can slope as little as one centimeter per meter/half an inch per yard, or you can increase this to as much as five centimeters per meter/two inches per yard if the area is very large. On the one hand, you make washing the floor down easier and also cut down the time it takes; on the other hand, you save water. Putting the drain-hole or channel at the far end from the door means the hose and your boots don't get dirty when you go in to clean up.

If you have only one dog, graveling the floor of the kennel or run with round river-gravel is a good and inexpensive option, but the dog may swallow some gravel. Grassed runs are pleasant to begin with but don't remain so for long unless they are very large. It's always difficult to clear the feces from the tufts of grass and the holes dug by the dogs. On top of that, your dogs will quickly trample grass into an unpleasant muddy mess. It's better to give them a smaller area that is easy to maintain.

A roof on a kennel run is not much use unless it is built against a wall that gives shelter from prevailing winds. Rain rarely falls absolutely straight down. If the enclosure is in a corner of the garden, it makes more sense to invest in a better quality kennel than to spend money on a roof. A useful fixture in an outbuilding is a self-filling automatic water trough to provide clean water, placed at a height where the male dogs cannot urinate in it. Fitted indoors, it keeps the water cool in the summer and prevents it freezing over in the winter. Failing that, a bucket hung on a chain will do. A galvanized or stainless dish is best for food.

As for the surroundings, a bushy hedge planted close by has the advantage of giving shade, but it does fill the kennel run with leaves in the autumn and can harbor insects. A bamboo screen or a plastic windbreak are good substitutes. They block the dog's view of what is going on outside and often reduce barking.

Feeding

*Good nutrition eliminates a lot of problems and keeps dogs
healthy and performing well in the field.
But you must choose the right diet for your dog.*

In the royal kennels of the past, dogs were fed a 'mash' which was based on a special type of bread or on cereal boiled in water. They were not regularly given meat until after the mid-nineteenth century. It's only in the twentieth century that our best friends' diet has gradually become more balanced, with the introduction of green vegetables, bonemeal and cod-liver oil.

A fuller understanding of dogs' needs has led to a burgeoning range of commercial products which provide all that a dog requires at every stage in its life. Experts in animal nutrition agree that dogs are more often overfed than well fed, and hunting dogs are no exception. Hounds are particularly at risk, as the owners of packs have a tradition of using every trick in the book to obtain food. Abattoirs have always been a good source of supply. If you go armed with the right permit, you can buy some parts of the carcass at a reasonable price, subject to health restrictions that may be in force from time to time. Paunches from cows or sheep are ideal, but udders and similar offal have little nutritional value for dogs. Other tripes need patience and the necessary equipment to clean them, but frozen tripe is available from all good petfood suppliers.

Feeding on a large scale

In poultry-farming areas, poultry abattoirs are also good places to get supplies. Chicken carcasses or, better still, duck and turkey necks are attractive on several counts: you can carry them away in a plastic bin, you can give them to the dogs just as they are, without any preparation, and they are rich in the fat needed by hardworking dogs. The disadvantage of all these sources of meat is the storage required. To feed a large

The modern petfoods now available take care of all your dog's nutritional requirements in a single meal.

Wonderful 'mashes' are still prepared in some hunting establishments, especially for packs of hounds.

pack you need a cold store, which is expensive to buy and maintain. For a few dogs, you can easily get by with a second-hand freezer or a reconditioned refrigerator with an icebox. But all this requires plenty of free time and suitable transportation, and often it simply isn't worth the effort. Leftovers from a school canteen are another possibility, except during vacations. If you live near a large trading estate, you can sometimes strike lucky and buy several pallets of dogfood at cut price because the cans are dented.

However, a hunter with several dogs or a pack is still likely to resort to the traditional method of preparing mixtures. The classic ones are made on a base of rice, barley meal, or maize, boiled in water to which fat or meat has been added. This well-balanced way of feeding has the advantage that you can vary the calorie content according to the season and the dogs' needs, simply by increasing or reducing the amount of fat you put in. But you do need a proper kitchen and large cooking utensils. Remember, too, that rice and cereals take a long time to cool down, which has to be allowed for on top of the preparation and cooking time.

Long live the dog biscuit!
Whether you keep a large number of dogs or only one, if you take the trouble to analyze the options objectively, you will find that in fact the best choice is dogfood produced by professionals to an appropriate formula for your dog. These products are the outcome of extensive research, often carried out in veterinary schools, and they offer an ever wider range in terms of both nutritional content and price. The cost is no longer an excuse to deprive your dog of the benefits of quality food, but you should be suspicious of incredibly low prices. The top brands prove to be more economical in the long run.

Finally, granules or biscuits are preferable to flakes that have to be soaked, and better than canned food. For one thing, dry food keeps well and is easy to carry. For another, the dog eats less of it and produces more compact and less evil-smelling motions – a worthwhile consideration.

Are food supplements necessary?

There are times in a dog's life when you must pay particular attention to its diet: for example, in very young puppies and brood bitches that are either pregnant or lactating. These critical periods in your friend's life are sufficiently rare for you to make that little extra effort. You will be amply rewarded.

Even then, the best choice is one of the whole dogfoods, preferably a top brand. You can also consult your vet, always the best advisor on nutritional matters.

Training for the hunt

The hunting dog is an athlete. You must keep an eye on your dog's physical fitness, which depends above all on plenty of exercise.

You won't keep a dog at a peak of physical fitness and confidence with a dish of food, the occasional pat and a few kind words now and then. When the day comes to join the hunt, the day on which you have pinned all your hopes, your dog's brilliant performance will fizzle out like a firework. You must get into training: both of you need all the winning cards you can get.

The abrupt close of the hunting season often marks the beginning of an enforced period of rest for a dog, which upsets its respiratory organs and digestion. It may put on about a quarter of its body weight, a critical threshold for its health. A good plan is to prevent this change in the rhythm of your dog's life by exercising it regularly all year round. It takes a long time for a strict diet to remove the excess weight, and it has a debilitating effect on the dog. Of course, you will have to adjust the balance of its food as well, but you must not neglect gentle exercise. It will do you as much good as your dog. When considering nutrition, do not be tempted by diet sheets. The usual formulated foodstuffs make rationing simple, thanks to their constant nutritional value. The price of these has come down considerably and they are easily affordable nowadays.

The best, and also the easiest, way to keep your dog fit is to take it for a brisk walk on the lead several times a week. At first, five or ten minutes will do, but make the walks longer as fitness improves. It is difficult to give precise guidelines, as needs vary considerably from one dog to another. So does the amount of free time available, but nothing should stop you taking a walk at all. You should start by taking exercise in small doses, to prevent your dog or dogs getting tired or out of breath. In spells of hot weather, try to take your walks in the early morning or late evening, if at all possible. Walking hardens the pads and makes your dog's feet less susceptible to cuts when galloping over fields of stubble or over scorching plowland.

Make the most of every outing

When the dog has built up sufficient lung-power and stamina, you can take it out behind your bicycle to improve its fitness. But do avoid setting your dog off in a straight line, for example along an avenue. Except for the exercise the dog takes at your side or at your heels, on the lead, a dog must run only to quest – that is, to search for game. Don't encourage it to become a sprinter, happy to nose out next to nothing. Worse still, it might empty the field of game right under your colleagues' noses! Hunter and dog are a team. Any time you spend together, particularly during exercise, gives you an opportunity to develop a better mutual understanding. One or two hours on a fairly regular basis will make your dog into an unrivaled hunting companion,

Going out with the bicycle at weekends is excellent exercise.

Packs of hounds used for hunting larger game are often taken out for an hour's walk behind the master or the whipper-in.

and your effort will be rewarded. From a purely practical point of view, you can't use a dog's skills and aptitudes to the full if you are not in control. Regular exercise sessions can be seen as a sort of 'honeymoon,' when you get to know and understand each other better. You will never make a dog obey you unless you are first able to make it understand.

The hunter can always learn from the dog by watching and listening to it, and working together aside from hunting makes for a calmer relationship, which is

a great advantage. Practical experience will teach you things you cannot find in books. This is blindingly obvious while out hunting, but proves to be equally true all year round. The little things that you find out for yourself and that stem from your own experience can make an enormous difference. In short, the time you devote to having a good dog is time well spent. As the old saying goes, 'the hunter makes the dog.'

How useful are artificial hunting enclosures?

What about the artificial hunting enclosures whose popularity is growing in many parts of the world? For example, there are 'captive hunts' in the USA, and 'game ranches' stocked with unusual and exotic species. The French have 'training parks' and other hunting enclosures ranging in size from some tens of hectares / around one hundred acres to several hundreds of hectares / about a thousand acres; they can even exceed a thousand hectares / 2,500 acres. Their existence reflects a growing demand from hunters. But how useful are they for you and your dog?

From the technical point of view, good quality enclosures of this type are rare. The majority are under 500 hectares / 12,500 acres, which is not a large enough

When most of the hunting enclosure consists of grassland, you can expect to find game concentrated in the thickets.

53

Do you need a hunting permit?

Legislation on hunting permits varies from state to state in the USA, but if you go after migratory birds you need a federal permit (tax stamp) on your state license.

Hunting permits are not required in the UK, but of course you must get a landowner's permission to hunt on their land. And you do need a license for your firearm.

area to allow game to behave naturally. Fencing limits the flight of game birds. It forces them to take the same route repeatedly, and to follow already beaten paths. This means that dogs are soon confronted by scent trails already covered by their own scent, which confuses them. On top of that, the pressure of daily or near-daily hunting puts every animal in the enclosure permanently on its guard. And if birds do manage to fly out of the enclosure, this makes it impossible for dogs to pick up their scent again and continue working correctly.

Despite such reservations, this type of facility can still provide a good way of introducing a dog to game. You can handle a dog there quite legally, and you can be pretty certain of finding game, so your dog's career gets off to a good start. The perimeter fence can even be seen as a safeguard for the dog: you can let it hunt more or less at will, but under observation, without fear of losing it. You can allow your dog to act naturally, to develop its own hunting style, and that is good. But don't let it get too used to these artificial conditions: they are rather different to those it will meet in the wild.

Don't confuse exercise and artificial hunting

The benefits of taking adult dogs to artificial hunting enclosures are less obvious. It certainly keeps them keen, but there is a risk that their skills could lose their edge. With frequent visits to facilities like these, dogs can start to lose their hunting instinct: finding game is too easy. The argument that such outings keep a dog fit isn't convincing: it's generally easier to walk your dogs close to home than to drive to a captive hunt. A dog's nose doesn't need exercise. You should be exercising the infrastructure, the dog's muscular system, and you can do that just as well on a road near your home as on open ground.

The type of game to be found in artificial enclosures is another consideration. How many animals there are and where they come from is vitally important. It's preferable to choose a facility where the game is scarcer, so that your dog really has to quest. But the most important criterion is the size of the enclosure. How much of the land can you actually hunt over? Some advertisements promise great tracts of land humming with game, but you later discover that they are partitioned into plots of around a hundred hectares/250 acres. This is disastrous: you should be able to range over the whole area.

Without condemning artificial hunting out of hand, it's worth giving detailed thought to what it offers. For example, in some enclosures of 1,000 hectares/2,500 acres and more the terrain is natural, but is parceled up. How large an area you need depends on your dog's breed and the type of game you want to hunt. Because of the way they behave, roe deer need a smaller range than wild boar. Rabbits are the best suited of all small game animals to hunting in an enclosure, but most of the hunts devoted to rabbits are unfortunately very small.

Artificially stocked enclosures are excellent places to introduce a dog to game: it's there in abundance.

Grooming

Many hunters think that grooming is only for cosseted lapdogs.
It is a pity that the care of some breeds, griffons in particular,
is often neglected nowadays.

Even a dog that lives in a kennel has the right to regular grooming. It's an aspect of elementary hygiene. Not only is it very good for the dog's relationship with its owner and for morale, but it makes the animal look better. If a dog's coat is neglected, it often smells most

The basic kit: a metal comb with a handle, thinning scissors, cutting scissors, stripping knife, and nail-clippers. A small bucket is useful to collect the hair.

unpleasant, especially when wet. It is a pity that the breed standard gives no information on grooming dogs. Some owners even seem to think that any effort they put into improving their dog's appearance will detract from its character.

Choose the right tools for your dog

The tools you need for grooming depend on the breed of your dog and, above all, on the type of coat it has. You want instruments that are up to the job, especially for wirehaired breeds.
A good basic kit consists of a metal comb with a handle, a pair of thinning scissors, a pair of cutting scissors, a stripping knife and a pair of nail-clippers. You should also have a small bucket for collecting the hair, which you should destroy for reasons of hygiene. It's best to groom your dog outside the kennel, and always choose the same place in which to do it.

Get your dog used to being groomed

It is a great help if you can teach your dog to put its forepaws on a stool. Young dogs submit easily to this routine with the help of a few tidbits. The comb untangles and combs out the hair. Never use it on a longhaired dog when the coat is wet, because the hair will pull out in clumps. The thinning scissors, just like the ones used by hairdressers, reduce the thickness of a mop without leaving unsightly scissor marks. Long cutting scissors with blunted ends are ideal for keeping fringes straight and tidy, and for cutting the long hairs some dogs have between their toes. The stripping knife is used to strip out dead hairs and tidy up the coat, giving it a lustrous finish. The nail-clippers need to be strong: the ones you use yourself aren't tough enough. When you cut a dog's claws, trim them level with the sole of the foot and no further. You can cause a painful injury by cutting into the quick.

Grooming wirehaired dogs

Smoothhaired dogs don't need a lot of grooming: you should just go over their coat with a brush and trim their claws. Wirehaired breeds and griffons need more attention. For example, well-groomed feet prevent them from looking clumsy and give them a perfect line, besides enabling them to move freely in the field.
During grooming, take a good look inside your dog's ears. Remove any dead hairs with your fingers and clean out the ears with cotton wool. You must consult

A good combing after the hunt is good for your dog, and outside the hunting season it's the only way to get rid of dead hairs.

a vet if you find any discharge: neglected ear diseases can become serious and difficult to cure. In the past, problems of this kind were regarded as a sort of collective epilepsy and the dogs were destroyed.

A good bath does no harm

Regularly groomed dogs scarcely ever need a bath. But if you want to bathe your dog, for example because it has parasites, watch the temperature of the water. A dog in full flight can plunge into a cold river and come to no harm, but you must be very careful with compulsory baths. The ideal temperature is between 30°C and 40°C / 85°F and 105°F, even in the summer. If your dog usually lives in the house, it's worth giving it regular baths. They make the animal less smelly and get rid of any ticks it may have picked up while hunting or out walking.

There is no need to purchase special bath products, but be careful about what you use. Never use very astringent household cleaners, which can damage a dog's skin and mucous membranes. Avoid perfumed products for the same reason. A gentle shampoo is fine, but traditional coal-tar soap is still the most suitable thing for dogs and is kindest for frequent use.

Ears are always vulnerable to infections and disorders. When bathing your dog, take the opportunity to wash the outer ear very gently or clean it with a paper tissue. Cotton buds are best avoided, and never insert anything into the ear canal.

Use a specialist instrument for cutting claws, to avoid crushing the nail with ordinary scissors.

Handling your dog or dogs in the field

Paradoxically, the best way to handle dogs during the hunt
is to give them as much freedom of action as possible.
This needs a lot of courage and a cool head.

Dogs are a bit like cars: to be in charge, you have to know how to steer. You need to have a certain feel for it. If you have the courage to let your dog give full rein to its eagerness and use its initiative, it will perfect the quest and will give you the greatest pleasure and excitement in the world. Through selective breeding, our dogs have become fearsomely efficient precision machines. With their great physical strength, speed, power and suppleness, allied to character and intelligence, they will quest far and wide.

Following the rules
Hunters whose pride is wounded and who are out of their depth may take it out on their dog, unless they know and follow the 'rules.' Everybody knows that when you miss a shot, it's the gun's fault!

Without going deeply into psychology, it is possible to lay down a few simple ground rules for good handling in the field. In the first place, when you are questing with your dog, you must be able to control your own excitement and keep calm. Hunting calls for careful observation and thought, which are incompatible with over-excitement. There is little point in teaching your dog discipline if you can't exercise it yourself.

Be discreet
'In general, a wise man observes a great deal during the hunt and speaks little and quietly to his dog.' This is how a famous hunter at the end of the nineteenth century summed up the best way to behave when hunting, whether you are out with a pack, a pointer, a spaniel, or a retriever.

Above all, don't follow your dog too closely, and never get in front of it, even if you see the game before the dog catches its scent or picks up its track. By staying behind, you can observe and assess the way your partner works. Watch as discreetly as possible. You will come to appreciate that only your own dogs can teach you how to hunt well and how to outsmart the game. It's the dogs that do the hunting, and very often you will do better to trust your dogs than your friends, or even yourself. We may have the brains, but they have the nose. The hunter must only intervene in the last resort, when the dog or dogs cannot sort out the problem themselves.

Choose your words and equipment carefully
The words you use to control dogs in the field must be clear and unambiguous. Your tone of voice is equally important.

Success in the field often depends on the handler's trust in his dog.

Dogs have a very good ear: they can distinguish between many different sounds and readily recognize the tone of a human voice. On top of that, they are usually extremely sensitive to being reprimanded by their handler. For all these reasons, the way you issue orders and the way you give encouragement must be clearly differentiated. To encourage your dog, use longer phrases, and speak very quietly, in a sing-song manner. By contrast, a command must be short and repeated several times in a firm tone that leaves the dog in no doubt. A horn for hounds and a whistle for other breeds are essential items in the hunter's kit. What they are made of, their size and shape, are a matter of personal taste, but they must produce a clear sound that can be heard from a distance. They are only used to direct the dogs, but it is useful if their sound carries well for the recall. In difficult terrain, you can also use the horn or whistle to maintain contact with the dogs without bringing them out of cover during a quest.

The recipe for good handling is simple: clear, succinct commands, reinforced by appropriate hand signals.

Pick a dog you can control

The adage 'like master, like dog' is apt. When you choose the kind of dog you want – and consequently the kind of hunting you are going to do – make an objective decision based on what you really want. Nowadays, there is a breed of dog to suit every hunter, something to cater for every taste. They come in all sizes and every color, and the range and speed of their questing varies just as widely. This is something people often ask about. Put plainly, there are very few really useless dogs, only hunters who do not know how to make use of their talents. So when you are deciding on a breed, try to make an honest assessment of your ability as a handler. All the evidence is that there are more good dogs than there is good hunting country, and perhaps that is the real key to the problem.

Dogs, even hounds, hunt more effectively if you handle them in a considered and restrained manner.

Post-hunt care and attention

The events preceding and following the hunt itself may appear secondary, but they are of prime importance, especially the care you give your dogs after the hunt.

You must examine your dogs as soon as you get home from a day's hunting or shooting. It's easy to see if one of them is limping, and you need to find out what is causing the limp. It could be a thorn, or a knock sustained on rocky ground. You must be alert to the possibility of snake bites at the start of the season. If the dogs have been hunting deer or wild boar, check that the injury is to the foot and not higher up the leg. Griffons in particular have long coats that can mask a wound caused by larger quarry. If necessary, give first aid by cutting away the hair around the wound and disinfecting it with surgical spirit. If the cut is deep, it needs veterinary attention as soon as possible, before it is too late to stitch it.

A little grooming boosts morale
After a hard day's hunting, especially through some types of vegetation, dogs may let their eyelids droop from tiredness. You must check that there is nothing in the eye. A dog that shakes its head or holds it on one side could have something lodged in the outer ear. If so, you must try to get it out, or seek veterinary help to avoid it going down into the eardrum. Dogs with blood on their jowls have usually bitten their tongue: this can look dramatic, but it is rarely serious. And it never does any harm to use a stiff brush on smooth-haired dogs or run a comb through the coat of the longhaired animals. It's a good way of getting rid of dead hairs. Finally, do praise your dogs after every hunt. Never let them feel like mere tools; show them that you think of them as valued hunting partners.

After the effort, comfort!
Remember to bring a container of water and a dish when you are hunting in a dry area. Dogs don't have much of an appetite after the hunt, but they do get thirsty.

At the start of the season, before the dogs are fully fit, you can give them a spoonful of honey. This is thought to guard against heart attacks. If they have to wait around, because you are not going straight home or to kennels, take care not to leave them in a drafty trailer. It's very bad for their health, particularly on rainy days when they come back wet. If you hunt regularly over the same land from a hut or a hunting lodge, a small area can sometimes be set aside for the dogs, with straw for them to nap in. They will welcome a nourishing, warm liquid meal a few hours after the hunt, but if you have fresh meat, always keep it for the next day.

Your dog needs plenty of fresh clean water to drink when the hunt is over, or when you take a break.

The role of the Kennel Clubs

Pedigrees, shows, working trials: there has never been so much interest in purebred dogs. How relevant is all this to the hunter?

The Kennel Clubs are the bodies that regulate dog breeding. They were organized by dog-lovers more or less all over Europe at the end of the nineteenth century. The British Kennel Club (founded in 1874), the French Kennel Club (established in 1882), and the Swiss Kennel Club (dating from 1883) are among the oldest of the national associations. Enthusiastic hunters, feeling the need to make a lasting record of their dogs' lineage, set up registers based on the system established in London in 1880. The American Kennel Club was founded in 1884. Known universally by its initials AKC, it is an organization of over 400 kennel clubs. Clubs are elected to membership by existing members. The Canadian Kennel Club consists of individual members elected after having served an apprenticeship period. There is a close relationship between the American and Canadian Kennel Clubs.

How important is a pedigree?

The Kennel Clubs try to promote the breeding and use of purebred dogs. They are patrons of shows and working trials. But above all they keep the registers and establish pedigrees. A pedigree is a record of a dog's ancestry. It is produced by the breeder and presented to the dog's new owner. More and more hounds have a full pedigree, containing their complete family tree and certifying that they belong to a so-called pure line.

But dogs without a known family tree can sometimes produce fantastic litters with great hunting ability. It's important to remember that the aim of breeding 'pure' strains is to produce similar dogs, with similar abilities in the field.

Pointing dog pedigrees usually show one or more 'trialers' in their ancestry, that is, champions in one of the various categories at field trials. This is not necessarily something to look for, but it does indicate the success of a line and increases the likelihood of getting an exceptional dog. Many spaniels come from imported parents whose pedigrees show the country of origin. But beware: a

In the Saint Hubert hound trials, the theoretical concerns of the Kennel Club coincide with the practical requirements of hunters in the field.

Aptitude tests assess the natural talents of a young dog.

Licensing dog shows is one of the best known functions of the Kennel Clubs.

bloodline that can be traced back to the country where the breed originated is no guarantee of outstanding hunting skills. There are non-working strains of hunting dogs in every country. The same is true for retrievers. And avoid high-sounding affixes: breeders choose them just to give the impression that their dogs are closely connected to the homeland of the breed.

More and more working trials

Many Kennel Clubs are patrons of field trials. There are various kinds of trials, catering for all forms of hunting and for every breed: hunting certificates for hounds, bloodhound trials, field trials for pointing dogs, spaniels and retrievers, tests in natural or artificial burrows and tests in cover for terriers.

There are national and world championships in numerous disciplines, giving rise to the multitude of initials that appear on dogs' pedigrees. The relevance of all this to practicing hunters is debatable. Trials should rather be regarded as guaranteeing the maintenance of high quality in the breeding stock. That was, after all, their original purpose.

Dog shows where individual dogs are judged against the standard of the breed remain the most popular and best known of the clubs' activities, as well the most accessible to ordinary dog-lovers. To take part, all you need to do is have your dog registered with the Kennel Club and enter it for the show in advance.

But take a bit of advice: if you want your best friend's behavior to live up to your expectations, prepare your dog beforehand for the new experience of spending the whole day at a crowded show, surrounded by strange dogs.

Names and addresses of national Kennel Clubs

USA
American Kennel Club, 5580 Centerview Drive, Raleigh, North Carolina 27606
Tel. 919 233 9767

Canada
Canadian Kennel Club, 89 Skyway Avenue, Suite 100, Etobicoke, Ontario M9W 6R4
Tel. 416 675 5511

UK
Kennel Club, 1 Clarges Street, London W1Y 8AB
Tel. 0171 493 6651

Our closest friends

For more than three hundred days in the year, most hunting dogs are also family pets. In some cases, they have no other role.

Labradors are number one among the hunting breeds chosen as family pets. They are also by far the most popular hunting dogs and the most highly prized as retrievers. Actually, only very few of their good qualities are used in hunting. Their good nature and quickness to learn have made them the supreme family dog. This is a paradox, because the breed was created for a hunting élite, and it has meant a radical change in the dogs' surroundings and way of life. When a breed goes from a small number of births a year to thousands, there is very little selection. The British have long been breeding labradors separately for beauty and for hunting ability, and this shows up in slightly different strains of dog. Labradors belonging to the working strain are usually lighter, more even-tempered, and faster. Labradors can do everything, but that is no reason to let them get away with doing anything they can. They are lively, fast, very intelligent dogs that learn very quickly, and bad lessons register just as well as good ones. Sound basic obedience training is often all that is needed to make them into good pets. They live 'through' their owner, always trying to please, and practice will do the rest. If they have a fault, it is their enormous appetite and greediness. Keen workers, they are rarely given enough to do and it doesn't take much overfeeding to make them fat.

The cocker spaniel and the Brittany spaniel

Cocker spaniels, the smallest and best known of the British spaniels, are delightful companions. At one time, their huge success as pet dogs in the United States and Canada was a cause of irritation to the breeders of the original strain, who rightly insisted on retaining the breed's hunting abilities. This resulted in the American cocker spaniel, which is bred purely as a pet. They are gentle, affectionate dogs in the home, growing very attached to their owner and the family, and preferring a comfortable sofa to life in a kennel. They are easy to look

The distinction and charm of some hunting dogs, like this Weimaraner, make them excellent family pets.

The miniature dachshund makes a perfect little companion.

after: regular brushing is all they require, unless you are going to enter them in dog shows. The long, floppy ears are the main problem. They are covered with long hair and trail on the ground, picking up grass seeds which can lodge in the ear canal. You have to keep an eye out for this. Cocker spaniels are greedy, even bulimic dogs and, like the labrador, tend to become fat if you don't take care to give them a balanced diet.

Brittany spaniels are also popular. They pack the 'greatest number of assets into the smallest space,' according to the breeders' motto. On car journeys, you can simply forget they are there. They are good company in the house, never a nuisance, docile and loving. Like all spaniels, Brittanys are given to spontaneous displays of affection.

How about a small hound?

Small hounds also make excellent companion dogs, especially bassets. The basset griffon vendéen is widespread in the United States and Northern Europe, particularly in Holland. The same is true of basset hounds, and most of them are kept solely as pets.

The French-bred basset artésien normand is lighter, less bulky and much more elegant. A widespread craze for them in the 1970s almost toppled them into the pet dog category. They have been the most common French basset for a long time and there are still a lot of them around. Their greatest practical asset is their character: these are gentle, placid, well-mannered dogs. Their ability to adapt to any circumstances makes them very popular. A rustic breed, and easy to look after, the basset artésien normand makes a pleasant fireside companion.

Terriers and dachshunds

The fox terrier is the hero of comic strip, animated film, and now television, thanks to Tintin's faithful accomplice Snowy. Cartoonists have spotted the breed's characteristic gait and made a fortune out of it. There are plenty of well-groomed fox terriers in fashionable circles, but although they can charm their way into a comfortable life, fox terriers have never lost their all-consuming passion for hunting. They are too talented to sit idle, and even when kept as pets they never become lapdogs. This is worth remembering if you want to avoid disappointment.

The dachshunds are also hunting breeds: compact, vigorous dogs with a familiar elongated silhouette. There are three breeds of dachshund, with two sizes in each breed. The miniature dachshund can fit into your shopping basket. And each size comes in various recognized colors: solid, bicolored, dappled, and brindle.

Breeds of
hunting dogs

Smoothhaired fox terrier

Tail carried high and straight

Straight, flat, smooth coat

Small V-shaped ears

Strong jaws and teeth

Strong bone structure

This expert terrier is also versatile and can hunt all kinds of game above ground.

Hunting skills

The smoothhaired fox terrier is the most popular of the terriers, with a smooth coat that is easy to look after. These dogs hunt all kinds of game equally well, from the smallest to the largest. They like scrub and excel at hunting rabbits in thickets and thorny bushes. They can even join in a pack beating for larger game, when they will take a particularly active part in the hunt.

General appearance

These are lively dogs and are immensely powerful in relation to their size, with a

TIPS

Training
Quick to learn and curious by nature, fox terriers take delight in going down burrows of their own accord. The affectionate puppy will obey at first just to please its owner, but does so later out of enjoyment. Training should be gentle and must not rely on punishment. But beware: fox terriers quickly pick up bad habits.

In town
These great sporting dogs enjoy a garden or yard but can also be kept in an apartment, though there's a risk of them causing damage if left alone. They need several walks a day. They are good guard dogs and affectionate companions, and get on very well with children.

perfectly balanced build. They have strong jaws with a scissor bite. The coat is white, and may have black, black-and-tan or tan markings.

Feeding

Fox terriers weigh only 8 kg/18 lb, and can be fed on a budget, needing just one meal at the end of the day. If your dog comes to the table to beg, give a small meal at midday. Increase rations during the hunting season.

Often specializing in difficult tasks involving narrow burrows, the smoothhaired fox terrier is nevertheless an attractive dog for anyone looking for a companion capable of almost any hunting job.

Wirehaired fox terrier

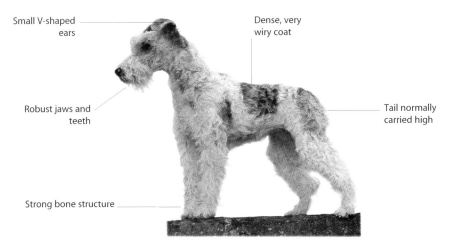

Small V-shaped ears

Dense, very wiry coat

Robust jaws and teeth

Tail normally carried high

Strong bone structure

This terrier is an expert burrower and its strong, thick coat is also an asset above ground.

A small dog of British origin, the wirehaired fox terrier is the one of the best known and most widely used terriers in the world.

16 in – they are very strong. They have round, deep-set eyes with an intelligent expression and a nose that is always black. The coat is mainly white with black, black-and-tan, or tan markings. The ears are V-shaped and a little thick. The neck is a good length and free from throatiness. They have a slightly sloping skull that narrows towards the eyes. The tail is carried high, and the back is level and strong.

Feeding

Needs are modest: one meal a day, preferably in the evening, is sufficient. If your dog comes to the table to beg, give a small meal at midday. Increase rations during the hunting season.

Hunting skills

Wirehaired fox terriers have a protective coat that makes them ideal for working difficult ground and tracking rabbits in thorny bushes. They have the same hunting skills as the smoothhaired fox terrier: they hunt all game equally well, large or small, and are used to hunt foxes underground. They can also join in beating for large game, and are particularly useful after wild boar.

General appearance

These active dogs have a well-balanced build. Although small – a male stands under 39 cm/

TIPS

Training
These lively dogs are a joy to teach. They are adaptable and quick to learn what is expected of them. They are also capable of carrying out a variety of tasks.

In town
At home anywhere, and can easily be kept in an apartment, so long as they are taken out regularly to relieve themselves.

German hunting terrier

Wiry or smooth coat with a good undercoat

Flat, broad skull

Tail carried high

Ears set high

*This is the only terrier that has never become a pet.
It is a versatile hunter and excels both above and below ground.*

*Like all the German hunting breeds, this terrier
can quest, give tongue on the track of an animal,
or find wounded game.*

chest. Their skull is flat, broad between the ears and narrower at the muzzle than the fox terrier. This powerful muzzle has a strong lower jaw. The coat is either wirehaired or smooth, and colored black, black and gray mixed, or dark brown, paling at the eyebrows, muzzle and chest. The eyes are small, deep-set and dark.

Feeding

These robust, light terriers are not big eaters. Give them about 220 g/8 oz of a dry whole dogfood a day.

Hunting skills

These versatile dogs can hunt above and below ground, give tongue, and quest on land and in water. They will track game into its den or lair and are invaluable on the trail of fox and boar. They are particularly fierce, unequaled at hunting by scent and unafraid of water.

General appearance

These small dogs (standing 40 cm/16 in to the withers) are longer than they are tall, and solidly built, with a straight back and a deep

TIPS

Training
These dogs are only suitable for hunters already experienced in training, who are used to handling strong-willed dogs. Once taken in hand, they will only obey their owner and are suspicious of strangers.

In town
German hunting terriers make good guard dogs and adapt well to life in a house or an apartment, so long as their owner shares their passion for hunting. Otherwise they become aggressive. Plenty of long walks are needed to let off steam.

Jack Russell terrier

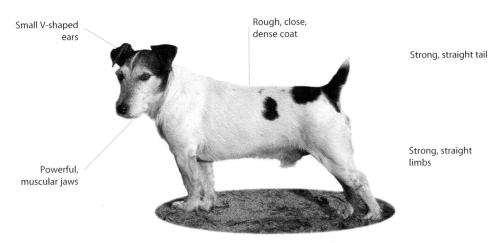

Small V-shaped ears

Rough, close, dense coat

Strong, straight tail

Powerful, muscular jaws

Strong, straight limbs

This expert terrier hunts foxes and works excellently in cover.
It is also a gentle and loyal companion that loves playing with children.

Hunting skills

Jack Russell terriers work particularly well in bushes and thickets. They are also used for hunting rabbits and other small game in its den or lair. Always persistent and courageous, these terriers are unafraid of wild boar, and can be used to hunt these and other large game.

General appearance

Jack Russells are small terriers, built for speed and endurance. The female stands only 33 cm/13 in and the male 35 cm/14 in tall. The coat is white, or white with flame, lemon or black markings, preferably limited to the head or the base of the tail. The rough coat is tight and dense, and can be either smooth or wiry. The skull is flat, with small V-shaped ears dropping forward a little and lying close to the cheek. The back is straight and the short tail is carried high.

TIPS

Training
Jack Russells are easy to train: they don't try to assert their personality like other terriers. Gentle, affectionate and courageous dogs, they need strict but kind and intelligent training if they are to live in the house.

In town
Can live in town but need at least an hour's walk every day, whatever the weather. You need a fenced garden where you can let them out for short spells, because these lively dogs are inclined to run off. They are friendly towards other dogs.

Feeding

Jack Russell terriers need to be fed a regular amount at regular times. They are fussy about their food, and you must make sure that they eat what they are given. They like tidbits, but be firm and don't let them beg at table.

A big star on the terrier scene, the Jack Russell combines good nature with formidable efficiency.

69

Irish terrier

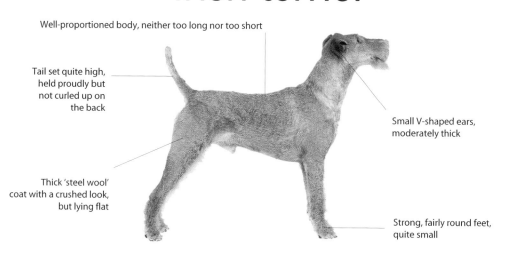

Well-proportioned body, neither too long nor too short

Tail set quite high, held proudly but not curled up on the back

Small V-shaped ears, moderately thick

Thick 'steel wool' coat with a crushed look, but lying flat

Strong, fairly round feet, quite small

The oldest of the terriers is an all-purpose breed: a farm dog, companion and guard dog, as well as a courser or gundog.

The Irish terrier won a great reputation during World War I, when these dogs were used to carry messages.

Hunting skills

This may be the oldest of the Irish terrier breeds. Its color was not fixed before the 1880s, and today there are black and tan and brindled ones, as well as the familiar red. The red variety was highly successful on its first appearance at English and American shows. The Irish terrier makes a good guard dog, courser and gundog: this is one of the best all-rounders.

General appearance

This dog has a lively and agile look, all muscle and sinew and strongly built. Its speed and stamina are just as important as its strength. The build should never be heavy, nor squat and compact, but with fine lines suggesting a courser's speed and elegance.

The Irish terrier has a flat skull, fairly narrow between the ears. The V-shaped ears, of moderate thickness, fall forward against the

jowls. The neck should be good and long, gradually widening to the shoulders. It is held well up, with no dewlap. The tail should have some substance and should be quite long and strong. The coat is very dense: it should not be possible to see the skin by holding the hair apart with your fingers. The color must be solid, and bright red, wheaten red or yellow red are the most sought-after varieties. There may sometimes be white on the chest and feet.

Feeding

This all-rounder should be fed according to how hard it's working, but needs no special diet. Some are gluttons, some a bit choosy: it depends on the strain and the size. The ideal ration, whether of commercial or home prepared food, depends on all these factors.

TIPS

Training
This is a dog with plenty of go and a strong character, but extremely loyal. Affectionate and good-natured, but brave as a lion when attacked, and never gives in. This breed's bad reputation is quite undeserved.

In town
Said to adapt to any circumstances, so town living is not out of the question. The coat needs regular brushing and three or four trimming sessions a year.

Welsh terrier

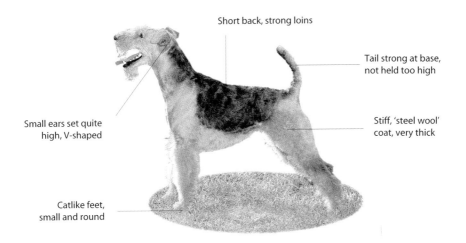

Short back, strong loins

Tail strong at base, not held too high

Small ears set quite high, V-shaped

Stiff, 'steel wool' coat, very thick

Catlike feet, small and round

Not used so much these days for hunting, but a good guard dog and pet, always on the go and easy to keep.

Hunting skills

This is a descendant of the Old English terrier (Old English black-and-tan terrier or Old English broken-haired terrier) and the fox terrier. Like its cousins, it has a natural bent for small game. In Wales, however, it has also been used in packs for hunting fox and even otter. Full of life, very courageous and cheerful by nature, it makes an excellent companion with good guard-dog qualities, though not aggressive.

General appearance

This terrier is quick, hardworking, well proportioned and compact. It has strong, muscular legs, with a good bone structure. The maximum height is 39 cm/16 in, and weight ranges from 9 kg to 9.5 kg/20 lb to 21 lb. The head is long, with a flat skull, a stop not too marked, and powerful jaws. The ears are V-shaped, carried forward and close to the cheeks. The neck is slightly arched and moderately long, the chest deep. It has an abundant coat; note that the absence of an undercoat is considered a fault. Color preferably black and orange, or black grizzle and orange, with no black penciling between the toes or black markings below the hocks. The tail is carried high.

TIPS

Training
Affectionate and obedient, the Welsh terrier is easy to handle. Start training early and be prepared for this dog, like all terriers, to be a little stubborn at times. Full of life and not shy, but not aggressive either. You will soon come to respect one another.

In town
This dog can live in town without any difficulty, so long as you take regular walks. Regular brushing is recommended for a good healthy coat, and it should be trimmed three or four times a year.

Feeding

This is an easy dog to keep. Once your dog is happy with one kind of food, there will be no difficulty with feeding. If you choose top quality biscuit, you will need between 170 g and 200 g/6 oz and 7 oz a day, but if you feed 'ordinary' biscuit or canned food, you should reckon on an average of 800 g/14 oz daily.

A Welsh terrier makes a good companion.

Smoothhaired dachshund

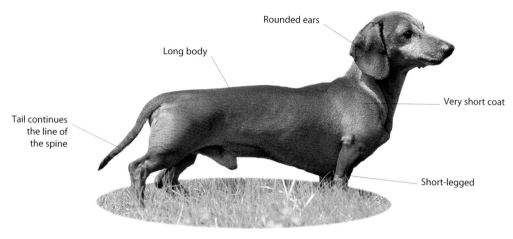

Rounded ears

Long body

Very short coat

Tail continues
the line of
the spine

Short-legged

The smoothhaired dachshund is the most common of the dachshunds and also the oldest, well known for its ability above ground and in burrows.

Dachshunds can share many aspects of the hunt with their owner. They are intelligent partners and willing to undertake any task.

underground. The coat can be solid (red, tan or yellow), bicolor (black or chestnut with tan markings), varied (shaded red, light gray or even white as the main color, with dark brown, dark yellow or black patches), or sometimes brindle.

Feeding

Never give in to those imploring eyes: dachshunds rapidly put on weight if you let them beg at table. The usual daily ration for a standard dog is about 190 g/7 oz of meat, but they need twice as much in the hunting season.

Hunting skills

Courageous and keen, dachshunds are all-round hunting dogs: they burrow, find wounded game, spring game and hunt in cover. Their main role is in tracking game. Their excellent sense of smell makes them useful for drawing foxes and badgers and for working in cover. There are two sizes: standard (9 kg/20 lb) and miniature (5 kg/11 lb) – very useful for getting down the smallest burrow or foxhole.

General appearance

The smoothhaired dachshund is the oldest of the varieties. Compact and close to the ground, these dogs must be neither too heavy nor too light. They have a long, tapering head with eyes placed obliquely. The ears are set high and well back, lying close to the cheek. The neck is strong and supple and the forelimbs very muscular, for working

TIPS

Training
Dachshunds are surprisingly independent, and the smoothhaired breed is even less submissive than the rest. But they are relatively easy to train.

In town
Town life isn't a problem, but smoothhaired dachshunds need long walks. They are likely to insist on going out: even if they live in an apartment, dachshunds don't usually grow slow and lazy. These dogs get on well with children.

Wirehaired dachshund

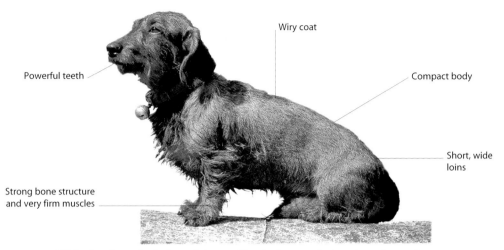

Wiry coat

Powerful teeth

Compact body

Short, wide loins

Strong bone structure and very firm muscles

This fearless dachshund is particularly good at going down burrows. It also makes a most pleasant household companion.

Hunting skills

Wirehaired dachshunds are expert at hunting wounded game. They also spring game well and work in cover. Bold, aggressive dogs that stand their ground, with a superb sense of smell, they are possibly the most versatile of the dachshunds and unequaled at hunting foxes.

There are two sizes of dachshund: standard (9 kg/20 lb) and miniature (5 kg/11 lb). The miniature dachshunds were bred for hunting rabbits and can get down the smallest of burrows.

TIPS

Training
You need to have some experience of dogs before taking on this variety of dachshund: wirehaired dachshunds are not the easiest to train.

In town
These dogs, although country-bred, can live happily in an apartment.

General appearance

Wirehaired dachshunds probably owe their distinctive appearance to crossbreeding between the smoothhaired dachshund, the schnauzer, the pinscher and the Dandie Dinmont. But the breed standard for all dachshunds is the same. Compact and close to the ground, they must be neither too heavy nor too light. They have a long, tapering head with eyes placed obliquely. The ears are set high and well back, lying close to the cheek. The neck is strong and supple and the forelimbs very muscular, for working underground. The coat can be solid (red, tan or yellow), bicolor (black or chestnut with tan markings), varied (shaded red, light gray or even white, with dark brown, dark yellow or black patches), or sometimes brindle.

Feeding

The usual ration is 190 g/7 oz of meat daily; any more than that and they get fat. Give twice as much during the hunting season.

Dachshunds have carved out a solid reputation for themselves as scenthounds and they are the most frequently used dogs for this purpose.

Longhaired dachshund

Muscular body

Long, silky coat

Ears set high

Firmly set limbs

The most refined dachshund is still a hunter at heart, but it is the variety best adapted to apartment life.

TIPS

Training
Be firm with these affectionate dogs. They will try to charm you by playing the fool, but longhaired dachshunds are not difficult to train.

In town
These refined dogs were bred for companionship rather than hunting, and apartment life suits them very well. The quietest and most affectionate of the dachshunds.

Hunting skills

These are excellent, versatile hunters in spite of their elegant appearance. They burrow, find wounded game, spring game and work in cover. They are bold, fierce dogs that stand their ground, with a superb sense of smell. Their small size is a handicap in snow and mountainous areas, so they are mainly used on level ground. The two sizes are standard (9 kg/20 lb) and miniature (5 kg/11 lb).

General appearance

These dogs differ from the smoothhaired dachshunds only in their coat, which is long, silky, flat and slightly wavy. Compact and close to the ground, they must be neither too heavy nor too light. They have a long, tapering head with eyes placed obliquely. The ears are set high and well back, lying close to the cheek. The neck is strong and supple and the forelimbs very muscular, for working underground. The coat can be solid (red, tan or yellow), bicolor (black or chestnut with tan markings), varied (shaded red, light gray or even white as the main color, with dark brown, dark yellow or black patches), or sometimes brindle.

Feeding

Never give in to those imploring eyes. The usual daily ration for a standard dog is 180 g/6.5 oz of meat and twice as much in the hunting season.

Dachshunds are friendly and agreeable at home and get on with all the family.

Basset hound

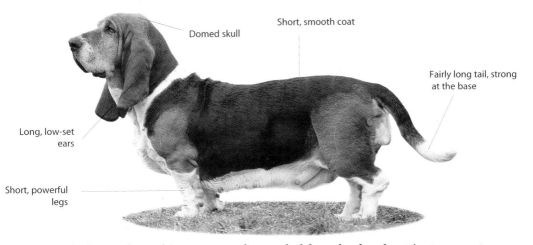

Domed skull

Short, smooth coat

Fairly long tail, strong at the base

Long, low-set ears

Short, powerful legs

The basset hound is very popular, and although often kept just as a pet, it is still an excellent hound.

Its outstanding voice and stamina make the little British basset hound a winner.

characteristic: medium-wide at the forehead, and tapering slightly towards the muzzle, which is clean-cut. The skull forms a dome, and the ears, set below the eyeline, are very long. The front legs are short, the body long and well let down, and the hindquarters muscular. The coat is tricolor (black, flame and white) or bicolor (lemon and white).

Feeding

Balanced feeding, whether you give home prepared or commercial food, is essential to good health and performance. You should reckon on 500 g/18 oz of meat daily in home prepared food, more in the hunting season. This hound may be fed once or twice a day, but there must be no snacks between meals.

Hunting skills

Selectively bred by English masters of hounds from French coursers, the modern basset hound is still regarded as a hare specialist. Fast despite its small size, it is equally skilled at hunting all kinds of large quarry, especially roe deer.

General appearance

This low-slung dog manages to be stylish as well as stocky. Not even a loose skin can diminish the elegant effect. The head is

TIPS

Training
Despite its strong character, this is a docile dog. It just needs a little time to understand what is wanted, and will then make a most loyal companion.

In town
The basset hound is often kept purely as a pet, and these dogs can be quite at home in an apartment. This doesn't mean that they lack spirit. Plenty of exercise is a must: basset hounds need daily walks, as well as the occasional longer outing, even outside the hunting season.

Basset bleu de Gascogne

Slightly domed skull, not very broad

Tail sometimes slightly feathered

Slight dewlap

Longish, conical ears

Strong legs, half turned out or nearly straight

A lover of hard going with a fine nose. Hunts hare as a specialty but also other game, large and small.

Hunting skills

The basset bleu de Gascogne is outstanding for its fine nose, good voice, and intelligence. It is above all a hare and rabbit specialist, but can be used as a gundog for all sorts of game. It comes into its own on difficult terrain, especially when dry. Some say it is a little slow, but it cannot be beaten for picking up the scent again when bad weather has confused the trail.

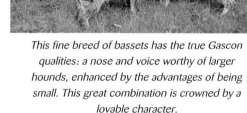

This fine breed of bassets has the true Gascon qualities: a nose and voice worthy of larger hounds, enhanced by the advantages of being small. This great combination is crowned by a lovable character.

General appearance

The basset bleu de Gascogne is similar in build to the grand basset bleu de Gascogne, except for its shorter legs. The head is clean, quite long, and pointed, with dark brown eyes and a somewhat wistful expression. The low-set ears are long, slender and conical in shape. The forelimbs are strong and straight, with muscular thighs. The very long back is held straight, and the fairly long tail, sometimes slightly feathered, is well anchored. The ample coat is blue, more or less extensively patched with black, with traces of flame. The coat may or may not have a saddle.

TIPS

Training
These are intelligent and affectionate dogs, and not hard to teach. They will respond to a gentle training program that progresses steadily.

In town
This breed can live in an apartment, unlike most hounds, but of course plenty of time must be set aside for letting off steam each day. Take longer walks at weekends, even outside the hunting season. Gets on well with children.

Feeding

You should reckon on around 300 g/10 oz of meat a day in home prepared food, or the equivalent in dry or canned dogfood. A balanced diet is important for health and effectiveness, so if you do prepare the food yourself, don't forget to supplement it with appropriate vitamins and minerals. These dogs need double rations during the hunting season.

Beagle

Powerful head

Short, thick coat

Strong tail, carried proudly

Rounded ears

The most popular of hounds, the beagle gets full marks on every count. Hunts anything, from large to small game.

Hunting skills

The beagle is the most popular of the hounds and, hunting aside, makes a very agreeable companion. Beagles usually work in a pack, hunting hare or rabbit, but they are beginning to be used more and more in drives for larger quarry. They have a very fine nose and great stamina. They are also very persistent: they will fight their way through bush and through briar to get what they're after.

General appearance

Beagles may look small but they can be stylish, even distinguished. They are certainly gay, lively and intelligent dogs, with an even temper. Standing at least 33 cm/13 in tall,

TIPS

Training
These dogs are easy to train and respond to a gradual and gentle approach, building up a stable and lasting relationship between dog and hunter.

In town
A very loyal dog, intelligent and affectionate, and a lovable companion. A beagle can live in an apartment and not be in the way, but needs a great deal of time for exercise.

their height never exceeds 40 cm/16 in. The short coat may have any of the appropriate colors for hounds, with the exception of liver. The tail is set high and carried proudly. Beagles have well-developed muscles and a powerful head. Their long ears are rounded at the ends. They are set low on the head and fall against the cheeks.

Feeding

You should reckon on 320 g/11 oz of meat a day in home prepared food, and more in the hunting season. Commercial dogfood is fine too, provided it is balanced. Food should not be given between meals, however great the temptation when you have the dog with you in the house.

Compact, with a powerful hunting instinct, the beagle is the most widely kept hound in the world.

Beagle harrier

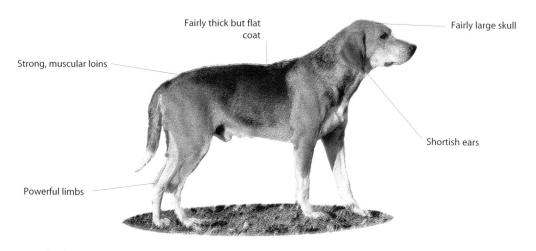

Fairly thick but flat coat

Strong, muscular loins

Fairly large skull

Shortish ears

Powerful limbs

The beagle harrier is remarkable as a hunter of hare and deer, and as a gundog, good on any terrain. It also makes an agreeable pet in town.

TIPS

Training
Beagle harriers are very gentle and loving dogs that need kind, gradual schooling to develop their talents.

In town
Enjoy living in an apartment, but need plenty of exercise. Beagle harriers make good pets; they get on very well with children and are friendly to other dogs they meet in town.

Hunting skills

Beagle harriers are used as hounds for small game and as gundogs. They are all-terrain dogs and can endure the worst weather conditions. Keen, with a harmonious voice and a fine nose, they also have staying power and speed. Beagle harriers marry the hunting skills of the beagle with the strength of the harrier. They were bred specifically for hare coursing, but are equally talented at the shoot and good after wild boar, roe deer and fox.

General appearance

Distinguished-looking dogs with pleasing proportions, beagle harriers have a fairly strong head with quite a broad, large skull, a slightly tapering muzzle and well-expanded nostrils. The eyes are wide open, with a frank and intelligent expression. The ears are not too long. They are V-shaped and hang almost flat. The chest is well let down. The limbs are strong, with very muscular shoulders and thighs. The back is short and level. Beagle harriers have a thick, flat tricolor coat (fawn with a black and white saddle), with bright, pale or dark shadings. Gray and whitish-gray tricolors are also recognized by the breed standard.

Feeding

Beagle harriers' demands are modest and they are not fussy eaters. You can feed them on home prepared food or commercial dogfood. They need 400 g/14 oz of meat a day, and increased rations in the hunting season. Avoid the temptation, which can arise when the dog lives in the house, to give them food between meals.

The beagle harrier is a very well-balanced dog, bred by hunters who demanded the best in both physical and mental qualities.

Harrier

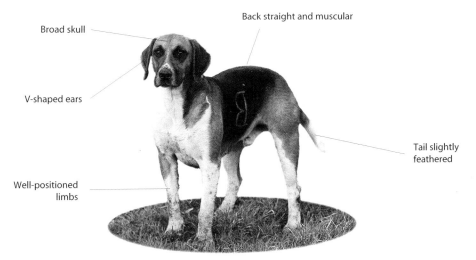

Broad skull

Back straight and muscular

V-shaped ears

Tail slightly feathered

Well-positioned limbs

Created for hare coursing, this breed is also useful after the fox. It is often used to improve bloodlines.

The harrier is a swift and distinctive hound bred in Britain. A good courser, always willing, slow to tire and well disciplined. It is suited to small game coursing and shooting, as well as being a most useful breeder.

Hunting skills

The word 'harrier' comes from 'hare.' The harrier was bred in England for centuries as a specialist hare courser, so this breed is smaller than the large hounds in its ancestry. It may also be used to hunt boar and fox, and combines well with other breeds in a pack. These are fast and hardy dogs, with an excellent nose, although not quite the all-rounders that many hunters look for. The breed is ideal for leading, and is also used for the improvement of bloodlines on account of its healthiness, good bone structure, stamina and speed.

General appearance

This is a strong dog, nimble and stylish, with a face full of character, a fairly long muzzle, a broad head and fairly large nostrils. The eyes are dark, small and oval, and the ears V-shaped, flat and pendant. The body is muscular, with a chest deep rather than wide. The tail is of medium length, slightly feathered and held high. The coat is flat, thick and not too short. It usually has a white background, with all shades from black to tan, often tricolor. The saddle is sometimes entirely black.

Feeding

Harriers are happy with home prepared food (reckon on 650 g/24 oz of meat a day) as well as commercial dogfood. The latter is often a better choice, as it is both cheaper and ready balanced. Harriers are easy to feed, but you have to watch for a tendency to put on weight.

TIPS

Training
These dogs need repetitive training, progressing steadily. This presents no problems so long as they are taken in hand early enough.

In town
The harrier is a rustic dog, suited to kennel life and crammed with energy. Does not adjust well to town life, unless there are wide open spaces nearby. Good with children.

Petit anglo-français

Short, dense, smooth coat

Long head, not too broad

Ears set low

Narrow, medium-length tail

Strong, muscular limbs

This hound combines the physical qualities of the English hounds with the finesse of the French, and is brilliant at hare coursing.

TIPS

Training
These obedient, confident dogs are not difficult to train. They are quiet and very receptive, and respond well to traditional training methods. Gradual schooling and kindness bring quick results.

In town
These may be gentle dogs, but they aren't pets and they don't take well to life in an apartment.

the forelimbs and thighs strong. They have a smooth, close coat which may be tricolor (white, black and flame), black and white, or black and tan.

Feeding

Feeding depends very much on how hard the dogs are working. During the hunting season, rations need to be doubled to 420 g/15 oz of meat a day. You can give an extra light meal before leaving for the hunt. Whatever the season, they need a balanced diet to stay healthy and perform well.

Hunting skills

These hounds bred for hunting small game are also useful as gundogs. A cross between French hounds and the beagle, this breed is the perfect compromise, combining the stamina of the English dog with the hunting skills of the French. With their speed and good nose, these are excellent dogs for hare coursing. This requires a range of sometimes conflicting skills, including resourcefulness and persistence on the scent. They are equally good at hunting roe deer, fox and wild boar.

General appearance

These well-proportioned, solidly built dogs have a long head, not too broad, with a slightly tapering muzzle. Their brown eyes have a gentle, alert expression. The petit anglo-français has open nostrils and soft, slightly folded ears. The chest is low and well developed, the back straight and level, and

The petit anglo-français is a French breed of hound, crossed with the beagle.

Grand anglo-français

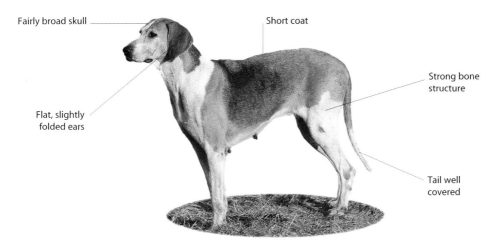

Fairly broad skull

Short coat

Strong bone structure

Flat, slightly folded ears

Tail well covered

This talented hunter of roe deer, stag and boar combines the scenting ability of the French hounds with the speed and fierceness of the English foxhound.

Even-tempered and powerfully built, the crossbred grand anglo-français hound is an illustration of the progress made in hound breeding during the course of the twentieth century.

Hunting skills

These are substantial, rustic dogs, at home on any terrain. They are the most widely used hounds for hunting large game. Though they have a less refined nose than the pure French breeds, they have an excellent sense of smell and knowledge of game.

General appearance

Like the chien français, the grand anglo-français comes in three varieties, with different coloring: the tricolor, the black and white (which is closest to the chien français in its coat and in its sense of smell), and the tan and white.

These dogs have a fairly short head, with a broad, flat skull and high-set ears, slightly folded at the tips. Everything about them seems to indicate power.

Feeding

These rustic dogs are not fussy about their food nor big eaters: they need 500 g/1 lb of meat a day or the equivalent in commercial dogfood. But this adds up to quite a large amount when feeding a hunt pack of some 80 to 100 dogs.

A balanced diet is needed for good health and performance, and the feeding of French grand anglo-français packs is usually based on the traditional 'mash.'

TIPS

Training

These loving dogs like people and pose no special problems in training. Kind, gradual schooling, without physical punishment, suits them best. It takes a little longer but is much more reliable.

In town

These dogs must live in kennels, not in town. They need frequent exercise, even outside the hunting season.

Chien français

Short, tough, close hair

Long, large head

Ears set in line with the eyes

Tail narrow, quite thick at the base

Strong bone structure

The chien français is proficient at hunting stag, boar, and roe deer, but each of the three varieties has its own character and hunting habits.

TIPS

Training
Chiens français are affectionate pack dogs that should be trained gently and gradually. They find their natural place in the pack depending on what they do best.

In town
These dogs naturally live in a pack and need an enormous kennel, with room to run about freely. They enjoy frequent outings, even outside the hunting season.

Hunting skills

These large, methodical dogs are experts at hunting stag, boar and roe deer. They follow the scent well and give tongue readily. They have speed and stamina, and are used almost exclusively for hunting large game. Each of the three varieties has different characteristics and talents, resulting from its origins.

General appearance

The three varieties of chien français are the black and white, with a large saddle or fairly extensive patches, the tan and white, and the tricolor, where the saddle can vary in size. The hair is short and quite fine. These are elegant, muscular dogs with good proportions. They carry their tail high, giving them an aristocratic look. They have an alert, intelligent expression. The rather long head has a large, slightly domed skull, well-developed nostrils and large eyes. The neck is long and strong, the chest deep and well let down. These dogs have powerful limbs, with strong, wide forequarters and long, muscular thighs.

Feeding

These rustic dogs are not choosy and are happy to eat either commercial dogfood or home prepared food. But a well-balanced diet is important, so if you prepare their meals yourself you must add the appropriate food supplements. Reckon on 500 g/1 lb of meat a day, and more when they are working.

Chiens français are the living embodiment of a centuries-old, very French tradition: the hunting of large game with hounds.

Poitevin

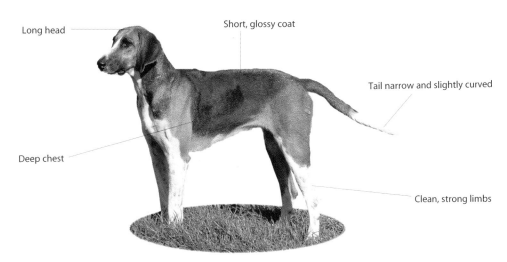

Long head

Short, glossy coat

Tail narrow and slightly curved

Deep chest

Clean, strong limbs

Considered the best dog in the world for hunting large game, this pack dog lives for the hunt and will pursue anything with legs.

Hunting skills

These aristocratic hounds hunt in packs. In the nineteenth century their specialty was wolf-hunting and they were famous for going through gorse. Nowadays these stylish hunters are first rate at hunting stag and roe deer. With their acute sense of smell, they can pick up a scent trail several hours old. Their exceptional strength enables them to bring game to bay, and they are so determined that no obstacle will stand in their way. This above all earns them their reputation as the best dogs in the world for hunting large game.

Its strength, elegance and lightness make the poitevin hound a distinguished and talented hunting dog.

General appearance

Poitevin hounds give an impression of power combined with grace. Their long head has a slight bump at the back of the skull. They have large, expressive, brown eyes, circled in black. The narrow, conical ears are set low, and the neck is long and thin. The Poitevin's short coat is tricolor with a black or white-and-tan saddle, or alternatively with large patches.

TIPS

Training
Even a born hunter like the Poitevin needs training. Give it a slow, gentle training program, and you will produce a well-balanced dog.

In town
These pack dogs are not really suited to life in town and should be kept in kennels. They need a kennel run that gives them enough room to gambol at will, and frequent exercise is essential.

Feeding

All these dogs ask is a balanced diet. They need 600 g/1.5 lb of meat a day, or the equivalent amount in dry or canned dogfood. Their requirements are greater when they are working, and you must increase their rations by half.

English spaniel

Thick, straight coat with some fringing

Wide, rounded head

No dewlap

Feathered tail

Muscular legs with good bone structure

This spaniel will find, flush and retrieve game on all kinds of terrain. Also makes a friendly and cheerful companion.

Hunting skills

This dog is just made for difficult ground. It doesn't set or point, but tears along, stirring up the game. This characteristic makes the springer spaniel a successful partner when hunting around prickly brush, ravines, ditches ... any place where the game has to be dislodged before it can be downed. Retrieving behavior also is completely instinctive.

General appearance

Longer-legged than other spaniels, the springer stands at least 50 cm/20 in, but is compact, neither too long nor too short. The skull is longish, fairly broad and rounded. It rises from the muzzle to a marked stop and is

TIPS

Training
The springer spaniel is biddable, but there's a lot for the handler to learn if the two are to work well together. This tireless, committed hunter isn't easy to keep with you: before you know it, the dog is beyond recall and has flushed the game up out of range. So long as the springer is taken firmly in hand, you will have no difficulty getting across what you want, because it doesn't lack intelligence.

In town
The springer, though bursting with energy, knows how to keep it in, but exercise is really essential. Home life suits this friendly and fun-loving dog, which really craves company.

divided by a vertical furrow between the eyes. The strong, muscular neck has no dewlap. The coat is liver and white, or black and white, sometimes with flame markings.

Feeding

A small dog, but nonetheless weighing some 20 kg/45 lb and needing a good bowlful to keep its robust build going. Make sure every meal is balanced: the quality of the food is as important as the quantity. A tendency to beg must be firmly countered.

A plucky little dog, ideal for the hunter who enjoys an exciting day's sport.

Cocker spaniel

Well-developed skull

Flat, silky coat

Ears set below eye level

Strong tail

Strong, compact body

*An all-terrain dog, good in cover, with a natural retrieving instinct.
At home, a friendly companion who will stay by your side.*

*This charmer makes a great pet, but is first
and foremost a skillful hunter of fowl and
furred game.*

Hunting skills

This breed was created, and named, for the woodcock, and it's a joy to see it painstakingly quarter the ground and flush out the most stubborn quarry. This dog will plunge unhesitatingly into long grass, through bramble thickets, and across rivers. No prey is safe, for this little spaniel can squeeze along the paths the rabbits use. Its coat protects it against furze. A good and instinctive retriever, too, even on marshy ground.

General appearance

This is one of the smallest hunting dogs (standing no more than 40 cm/16 in tall) and among the most appealing, with its cheerful demeanor and its gentle, intelligent brown eyes. The head is characteristic, with a square muzzle and a stop halfway between nostrils

and occiput. The skull is well developed, and the ears, set in line with the eye, are magnificently fringed. The legs are short, and the chest full. The loins, though not long, are broad. The rather short, glossy coat may be black or black with flame, red, cream, golden, chestnut, chestnut with flame or multicolored.

Feeding

This spaniel is a hearty eater, and will soon devise all sorts of dodges for getting an extra treat. But it doesn't need a lot of food, and will put on weight if not exercised enough. During the hunting season, though, double rations are needed – after work is over.

TIPS

Training
A very intelligent dog, quick to get the hang of what's wanted. But firm training is needed, or this one will go into business on its own account.

In town
This bundle of energy will be happiest if there is a garden at hand. Can take to apartment life, but needs frequent walks.

Swiss hound

Tail set in line with hindquarters, medium-length and narrow, lightly curved up at tip

The whole line from neck along back to tail should be harmonious and held well up; back firm and straight, loins muscular

Ears set above the eyeline and well back, never widest at the base, very long and pendant

Rounded feet, close-set toes; hard, rugged pads; strong nails matching coat color

Short, smooth, thick coat, very fine on the head and around the eyes

A confident, independent-minded quester and locator of game on any terrain.

Hunting skills

The Swiss hound is of very ancient origin, being recorded in Roman times among the Helvetii. It was a breed much prized by the Italians in the fifteenth century, and by the French in the eighteenth, for its superlative skill in the difficult art of hare coursing. Breeding in its native country has been enriched by strains of French hounds brought back to Switzerland by mercenaries. A standard for each of the five 'forms' was established in 1882, and these were revised in 1909, with the dropping of the Thurgau hound. On 22 January 1933 a single standard was established for all four varieties. This small game dog is used as a gundog, and is generally set after hare, deer, fox and occasionally boar. It thinks for itself as it hunts, and gives voice continuously. Even on difficult ground it has a sure touch in questing and starting.

General appearance

This is a breed of medium height, with a good build which promises vigor and stamina. A long muzzle and clean head with long ears give the Swiss hound an aristocratic air. The skull is long and narrow, with a clean line. The muzzle is roughly the same length as the skull. The chest is deeper than it is broad, and well let down, at least as low as the point of the elbow. Coat color differs from variety to variety:

- Bernese hound: white with black patches or saddle. Light to dark tan markings over the eyes, on the jowl, inside the ears and around the anus

- Jura brown: tan with black or sometimes dark gray saddle, or black with tan markings over the eyes, on the jowl, around the anus and on the legs
- Lucerne hound: blue, an effect that results from close mixing of black and white hairs; very dappled, with black saddle or patches. Light to dark tan markings over the eyes, on the jowls, on the chest, around the anus and on the legs. A black coat is allowed
- Schweizer hound: white with tawny orange saddle or patches, and occasionally very slightly mottled. A tawny orange coat is also allowed.

Feeding

This dog is prized for its rustic simplicity, and is not at all difficult to feed. Increase rations in cold weather or during the working season. How much food you should give depends on the dog's weight and height, and you need to keep a close eye on your dog.

TIPS

Training
This dog is gentle, biddable and will grow very attached to you, but needs firm training from the start.

In town
Needs space and exercise. Keep the coat in good condition with regular brushing.

Austrian hound

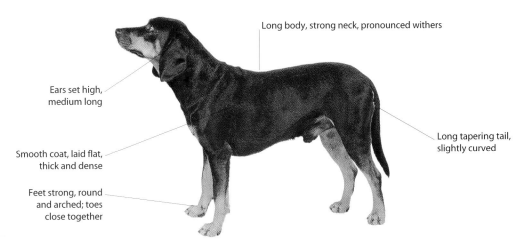

Long body, strong neck, pronounced withers

Ears set high, medium long

Smooth coat, laid flat, thick and dense

Feet strong, round and arched; toes close together

Long tapering tail, slightly curved

With the capabilities of a runner and a tracker, the Austrian hound really shows its mettle when the going gets tough.

Hunting skills

This dog is thought to be a true descendant of the Celtic hound, though as with almost all ancient breeds there is no absolute proof of its existence before the mid-nineteenth century. This hound of medium height is not widely kept outside its native Austria. An excellent sense of smell makes it particularly well suited to mountainous country, and it is also good on level ground. This breed's special talents come to the fore in difficult conditions. It tracks hare with particular confidence and has a good voice, with a shrill cry. The Austrian hound is regarded as a good runner and is equally highly valued as a bloodhound.

General appearance

Of medium height and solidly built, this dog is also long and supple. The skull is wide, with a strong, straight muzzle and large but neat

chops, uniformly colored. The ears are rounded at the tips and fall flat against the jowls. The neck, medium long and ideally without dewlap, is extremely strong. The dense coat is about 2 cm/1 in long, smooth and laid flat. The hair is thick and soft, with a silky sheen. The color is black with only a few flame markings, outlined in a light to dark tan. The two flame marks over the eyes (giving the dog its nickname 'four-eyed') must be present.

TIPS

Training
Training this good-natured dog presents no problems.

In town
Likes plenty of space to run around, so happier in the country. Regular brushing will keep the coat in order.

Feeding

Either dry or canned whole dogfood or, if you prefer, home prepared food will do for this unfussy dog. Extra rations are needed in the working season, to give extra energy when the dog is working harder.

A friendly nature and an excellent nose make the Austrian hound a good pet as well as a fine hunting dog.

Tyrolean hound

Strong body, long harmonious lines

Long tail, set high

Strong feet with close-set, well-arched toes and hard-wearing pads

Broad ears set high, with rounded tips

Coat on the coarse side; good socks on thighs

The ideal hound for forest and mountains.
Unbeatable following a trail, or to start a hare or fox.

Hunting skills

The Tyrolean hound is a descendant of the ancient Celtic hound. With its double coat of hair, this is a classic among the hardiest breeds of hunting dog. It was used as early as 1500 by the Emperor Maximilian I in the Tyrol, and we learn from his hunting books that he chose these hounds for tracking game. Modern breeding began in the Tyrol around 1860 and the standard was drawn up in 1896. The breed has been recognized since 1908. Of the many ancient strains of hound used in the Tyrol, only the tawny and black-and-tan varieties have survived.

This is an ideal all-round dog for forest and mountain hunting. The dogs are used singly to start hare or fox, or to seek out any kind of wounded game. This dedicated hunter is endowed with a very fine sense of smell. It quests and starts for love of the chase, and never tires. The cry is piercing and prolonged. The Tyrolean hound also has an excellent sense of direction.

dewlap. When the dog is excited the tail is carried high, but it may be curved like a saber. Tufted tails with stiff hair are much in demand. The thick, bristly coat is tawny (red, deer-colored, tan) or black (saddle black, with ill-defined red markings on the limbs, chest, abdomen and head). There are also tricolored individuals.

General appearance

This is a hound of medium height, with a solid bone structure. All small individuals were excluded from the breed in 1994.

This breed has strong muscles and sinews, and is robust and healthy. It would fit into a rectangle, being slightly longer than it is tall. The large skull is neat and slightly rounded. Draw the ears forward without forcing, and their tips should reach the canines in the upper jaw. The neck is quite arched, neither scalloped nor too floppy, and clean, with no

Feeding

In the hunting season this dog needs extra rations, but normally dry or canned dogfood will be fine, unless you want to go in for fancy cooking. Preparing your own food is more of a chore, as you must make sure that the diet is balanced. Give just one meal a day, in the evening.

Slovakian hound

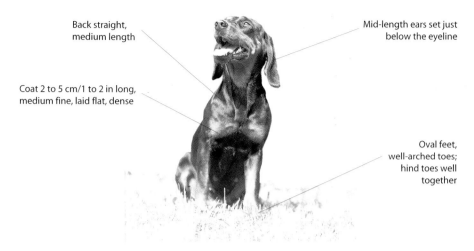

Back straight, medium length

Mid-length ears set just below the eyeline

Coat 2 to 5 cm/1 to 2 in long, medium fine, laid flat, dense

Oval feet, well-arched toes; hind toes well together

This breed has a great reputation as a determined follower of a trail or a fresh scent, never tiring or getting lost.

Hunting skills

The Slovakian hound is an old breed, probably descended from the ancient hounds found in Eastern Europe in the earliest times. This dog has an excellent nose and can follow a trail or a fresh scent for hours, without tiring, while keeping up a good cry. Also noted for its well-developed teeth and excellent sense of direction. That is why this hound is used in its country of origin for hunting wild boar and other dangerous game.

General appearance

This dog is quite light in build, but with a solid bone structure. The male stands 45 cm to 50 cm/18 in to 20 in at the withers, the female 40 cm to 45 cm/16 in to 18 in. The weight ranges from 15 kg to 20 kg/33 lb to 44 lb. The body is shaped like an elongated triangle, due to the broad and well developed chest. This characteristic makes the Slovakian hound ideal for bringing down a wounded quarry. The ears are rounded at the tips and covered with short hair. They are held close to the head, which is large by comparison with other hounds. The muzzle is also fairly large and slightly pointed, and the nose is always black. The strong neck, although short and muscular, is well proportioned. It should ideally be clear of dewlap, and without any loose skin.

The coat is always glossy black in color, with patches of red or tan. As is typical of hounds, these markings are never dark brown. They appear on the eyebrows and lower jaw, on parts of the throat and abdomen, and on the feet and lower parts of the fore and hind legs. The undercoat is very thick, especially in the winter, but it should be present in the summer too.

This is a fine-looking dog, giving the overall impression of a powerful, robust and well-proportioned animal. It is stronger than the Austrian hound, for example. The Slovakian hound has an even temper which, allied to remarkable courage, makes it an ideal companion for hunters of large game, as well as an excellent guard dog.

Feeding

This is a rustic breed, and not difficult to feed. Allow 500 g/18 oz of meat a day on average, and give just one meal a day, preferably in the evening. Some breeders maintain that rations should be adjusted in proportion to the dog's size.

TIPS

Training
Firmness should be used in training. This breed makes a good guard dog, but with its lively temperament is not really suitable as a pet.

In town
At home in the country and needs a lot of exercise. Easy to look after: just brush down now and then.

German spaniel

Long body; strong neck without dewlap

Coat long, tough, thick and wavy; may be slightly curly or flat

Ears set high, flat, not curled, and not too long or thick

Powerful legs

This is a courageous dog and an all-terrain hunter of small game and vermin. Good at retrieving also.

TIPS

Training
This hunting dog also makes a good companion, but needs firm training right from the start.

In town
Needs open space and exercise. This spaniel doesn't find apartment life difficult, but it's certainly no lapdog. Keeping your dog's coat in good order is simple: give it a regular brushing, and make sure you check its ears often.

Hunting skills

The breed was created around 1890 by the German breeder Frederick Roberth. A number of small and medium-sized longhaired hunting dogs were involved in the crosses. Specializes in small game and is a good choice for dealing with foxes, as well as larger quarry. It stops in the presence of game and alerts the hunter by its 'set.' It also has good retrieving capabilities, including skill in finding wounded game.

General appearance

This spaniel weighs on average 20 kg/45 lb. The male stands 48 cm to 54 cm/19 in to 21 in at the withers, and the female 45 cm to 51 cm/18 in to 20 in. The body is definitely long, the chest deep and well let down and the abdomen fairly high. The muzzle is wide and robust, with large brown nostrils. The coat is either deep brown all over, or shades of fox-red and rowan-brown with patches of brown and white, mottled, or tricolor.

Feeding

Not a greedy dog. Whether you choose home prepared or commercial food, allow 500 g/ 17 oz of meat on average. One meal a day is best, preferably in the evening, as for any self-respecting hunter. But make sure the diet is well balanced, and remember to feed more in the working season.

The German spaniel is daring and brave, with a reputation as an untiring worker on any terrain. Best suited to questing in woodland, with a good voice.

German shorthaired pointer

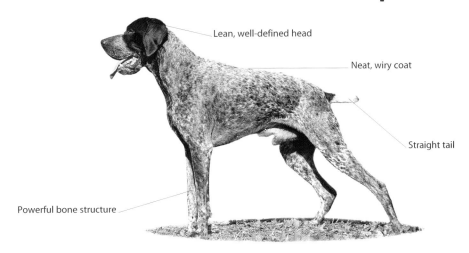

Lean, well-defined head

Neat, wiry coat

Straight tail

Powerful bone structure

The German shorthaired pointer excels in all kinds of hunting and makes a splendid companion.

Hunting skills

This is a powerful dog, and one of the best for practical hunting. It is favored by hunters for its all-round skills, which make this pointer equally at home in the thickest cover and the most open country. You will find this highly effective and deservedly popular breed at work on all kinds of terrain. Not many of the European gundogs can rival the British breeds, but this one can, whether in the hunt or in competition.

General appearance

This elegant and powerful dog has well-balanced lines. The head is clean, the flat ears set below the line of the eyes. The neck is long, with no dewlap, and the loins are short, with broad, muscular hindquarters. The back is straight and the chest long and well rounded. The short coat can be chestnut with no markings, chestnut with small white patches or chestnut blotches, light brown roan, or white with chestnut markings on the head. Height 58 cm to 65 cm/23 in to 26 in.

TIPS

Training
This is not a hard dog to train, though independent-minded and perhaps a little more stubborn than the French pointers. Just assert sufficient authority to take charge. You can really trust this well-balanced dog to react with moderation. Not in the least aggressive, timid, or highly strung.

In town
A good companion, well-mannered, obedient and cheerful. Needs lots of walks when the season is closed for hunting.

Feeding

This pointer needs a lot of food, especially during the hunting season, when you should give double rations. Make sure every meal is balanced. Dry whole food is relatively cheap and is formulated to provide all the necessary nutrients: this is perhaps the best option.

A courageous and effective pointer, this German breed has gradually become the most widely kept and popular of the gundogs.

91

Small Münsterlander

Thick, slightly wavy hair

The distinguished head of a thoroughbred

Wide ears, set high

Deep chest

Feathered tail, turning up slightly

An energetic gundog, comparable with the smaller spaniels.

Hunting skills

Quite similar to the Brittany spaniel, and makes an excellent hunting dog. In France these dogs are mainly used after rabbit. In Germany they take part in full trials which require them to show skill in pointing (with fowl or furred game), retrieving, tracking and water work. They are at home in open country, woodland, or marshes, and have a very fine sense of smell. Despite its active questing behavior, this breed doesn't leave the hunter far behind. Also used as a gundog, it possesses the talents of both spaniels and pointing dogs.

This powerful little brown and white spaniel combines strength with great dignity and more than a little elegance.

General appearance

This elegant spaniel stands 50 cm to 56 cm/ 20 in to 22 in at the withers. (The large Münsterlander stands 60 cm to 62 cm/24 in to 25 in.) The head is elegant, with a smallish skull and a pronounced stop. The strong muzzle is long and straight. The wide ears, set high, fall close to the head. The chest is deep, the feet straight and feathered. The well-feathered tail is held horizontally. The coat is brown and white or brown/roan; the hair is medium-length, flat and slightly wavy. The eyes are dark brown, the darker the better.

TIPS

Training
A willful dog, needing a firm approach, but a good pupil because of its great intelligence. Training needs to be methodical, with detailed work at every stage.

In town
Good-natured and affectionate with the family. Does well in town, though it helps if there is a garden for letting off steam. If not, regular walks will keep this dog happy.

Feeding

These dogs are moderate eaters, needing only 300 g/10 oz of meat a day in home prepared food, and about twice as much in the hunting season. Commercial dogfood, formulated to provide all the dog's requirements at any age, is just as suitable.

German longhaired pointer

Fairly long head

Robust, muscular body

Wide ears with rounded tips, set high and falling flat against the head

Long hair, laid flat

Feet moderately long and rounded, with well-knit toes

Tail strong at base

This large dog with its quiet temperament can adapt to every hunting style and never shows the least sign of tiring.

Hunting skills

It's not clear how this breed, called simply 'Langhaar' in its native Germany, began: some say it was with a cross between the German and French spaniels, with a little of the Irish and Gordon setters thrown in. It has a reputation as a fine nose, and can adapt to any style of hunting. Always shows great interest in the hunt and remains calm. Despite these good qualities, the breed is not widely known outside Germany.

This unflappable and persistent dog is a useful pointer.

General appearance

This pointer has a robust and muscular body, yet it still gives an elegant impression with its fine silhouette. The neck is sturdy but aristocratic, continuing the lines of chest and shoulders with elegance. The head is long and clean, in proportion with the dog's size and with skull and muzzle of equal length. It moves at a fast but unhurried pace. The coat is chestnut in color and the hair some 3 cm to 5 cm/1½ in to 2 in long on the back and sides. The hair on the neck, chest and abdomen is a little longer. The legs must have a proper comb, with the fringing getting shorter toward the feet.

Feeding

Not a very demanding dog: adults can be fed just once a day. What really matters is a well-balanced diet, so it's probably best to use commercial dogfood, which is easy to measure out and to serve.

TIPS

Training
This is an obedient, pliable dog, and not easily upset. There should be no particular difficulties in training, for the dog is eager to please and very loyal.

In town
Needs space and exercise, and must be given a daily walk to let off steam. Regular brushing will keep your dog's coat in good condition.

Picardy spaniel

Broad, domed skull

Brown nose

Coarse coat, not glossy

Good bristly tail

Broad, deep chest

This versatile breed is equal to every task the hunter demands of it, and deserves to be better known.

TIPS

Training
The Picardy spaniel is easy to handle and not a problem to train. Even inexperienced hunters can cope with this keen, intelligent dog. A good pupil that will learn quickly, given gentle treatment.

In town
Doesn't need a lot of room and can be kept in town, but – like all hunting dogs – enjoys wide open spaces. An obedient, gentle dog, affectionate toward its master and with children.

at the withers, its back rising towards the tail. The head is long, with an oval skull and a long muzzle. The line of the nose is slightly hooked and the slender flews hang well down. The low-set ears are long and feathered, the neck clear of any dewlap. The feathered tail is carried low when hunting.

Feeding

These dogs aren't fussy eaters. Reckon on about 400 g/14 oz of meat a day, and twice as much in the hunting season. Commercial dogfood is perfectly suitable. Picardy spaniels will put on weight if allowed to beg at table.

Hunting skills

This robust, hardworking spaniel is an all-rounder, suited to any terrain and capable of plunging through bramble thickets. Good in open country and woodland, but excels on marshy ground, because it doesn't shirk the water and retrieves well. The Picardy is a skilled hunter of woodcock, which can only be said of the very best pointing dogs. It is methodical and determined, with plenty of stamina. This breed is a favorite of French hunters.

General appearance

The Picardy spaniel has a grayish-white coat with brown patches. Stands 55 cm to 60 cm/ 22 in to 24 in

The Picardy spaniel shows outstanding courage and endurance under testing conditions. It was bred for the marshes and coppices of its native Picardy, where the climate is cold and damp.

Brittany spaniel

Rounded skull

Short back

Short, high-set ears

Short tail, tufted at the end

Deep chest

The most popular of the French pointing dogs, no doubt due to its extraordinary effectiveness as a hunter.

Hunting skills

The Brittany spaniel is a real 'Jack of all trades.' This liveliest and quickest of the French pointing dogs excels after all kinds of game, fowl or fur, and on all sorts of terrain, including marshy ground. It is a natural finder and retriever of game, with the stamina to go out day after day. It is also excellent after woodcock, which puts it among pointing dogs of the first rank, since this quarry requires a very fine nose, initiative, and above-average hunting skills.

General appearance

Quite squat in appearance, the Brittany stands only 46 cm to 51 cm/18 in to 20 in at the withers. An elegant and intelligent-looking dog, its quick reflexes and enormous energy make it a good partner in the field. It has a 'cobby' shape, short and compact. The muzzle is straight or slightly ram-shaped. The ears are

TIPS

Training
Loving and eager to please, Brittany spaniels are highly trainable. They learn fast and retrieve instinctively. Some individuals may be more difficult than others, but with a little insight it won't be hard to get across what's wanted.

In town
These dogs make excellent companions for the town-based hunter. They take up little room and get on well with people, especially children.

short and triangular, set high and slightly feathered. The Brittany has a shorter coat than other spaniels, flat to the body. It can be white and tan, white and chestnut, white and black, tricolor or roan. The tail is short, about 10 cm/4 in. Some are born tailless, and in France the others are always docked early on.

Feeding

This little dog isn't a big eater. Reckon on about 300 g/10 oz of meat a day in home prepared food, and double in the hunting season. Brittany spaniels are not fussy, and will eat commercial dogfood, dry or canned.

Perhaps there's no such thing as the perfect hunting dog, but the Brittany spaniel, the world's only pointing spaniel, certainly holds its own against all comers when it comes to locating feathered game.

French wirehaired pointing griffon

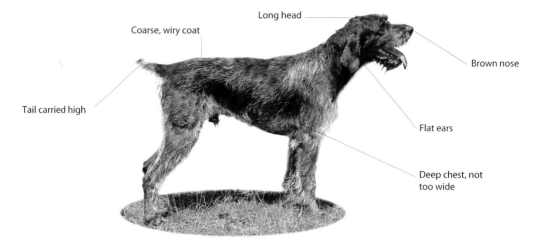

Long head

Coarse, wiry coat

Brown nose

Tail carried high

Flat ears

Deep chest, not too wide

This dog was bred for all tasks, in any weather and on any terrain.
It's a well-mannered and affectionate companion into the bargain.

Hunting skills

This tough, rustic breed has a protective shaggy coat. It specializes in marshy ground, but is also useful in thick cover and favored by shooters of woodcock. Gives a good account of itself in open country also, and is steady at the point. An unbeatable retriever, and deservedly the most popular of the pointing griffons.

General appearance

The thick coat, rough but not frizzy, betrays the breed's country origins. It has an engagingly intelligent manner. The long head is covered with short hair, apart from the mustaches and thick eyebrows. The muzzle is quite long and broad, and the nose a little hooked. The medium-sized ears are flat, the

This breed keeps close to the hunter and is completely committed to the quest. Skillful and courageous, and now indispensable to some on account of its really tough coat.

TIPS

Training
This dog may look rough, but is in fact friendly, docile and easy to train, asking nothing better than to be taught the hunter's craft.

In town
Lives happily in town, provided it gets frequent exercise. The perfect pet: affectionate, well-mannered and sociable.

neck clear of any dewlap, and the chest deep. The coat may be gray-blue with brown, brown all over, or white with a lot of brown. The eyes are large, with deep yellow or blue irises.

Feeding

A moderate feeder with rustic tastes, quite happy with either home prepared or commercial food. Reckon on around 430 g/ 15 oz of meat in home prepared food, and give twice as much in the hunting season.

German wirehaired pointer

'Steel wool' coat

Ears set high

Tail well covered

Clean, vigorous limbs

This is a good all-rounder that needs fairly constant training, but makes a really delightful living companion.

Hunting skills

This pointer is all virtues, and has become the standard by which the Germans measure a hunting dog. It is also highly appreciated elsewhere, and may even be the most popular of all pointers. Full of energy and determination, this dog enjoys the water and is prepared to jump in whatever the weather. The shaggy, wiry coat is ideally suited to difficult terrain, such as forests and mountain slopes.

TIPS

Training
An excellent hunting dog, provided training has been thorough. This needs a little patience and skill, but is not a daunting task because these dogs make receptive pupils.

In town
A dog to have in the house, so long as you make sure it knows its place.

General appearance

A stylish pointer, with an energetic and lively temperament. The coat, hard and bristly like steel wool, gives it a rustic look. The color can vary from dark to mid-brown, or may be chestnut mixed with white or light brown, or gray flecks. The eyes are dark and limpid, the face clean. It stands 56 cm to 67 cm/22 in to 27 in at the withers. The head is of medium length, with a strong jaw, a neck clear of any dewlap, and mid-length, pendant ears, set high. The back is short and straight, with broad hips and sloping shoulders. The breed has long hindquarters, short turned-in flanks, and a short tail.

Feeding

This is a fairly heavy feeder, especially during the hunting season, when rations should be more or less doubled. A balanced diet is necessary for health and effectiveness.

A well-built and versatile gundog, the German wirehaired pointer is first and foremost a practical hunting dog.

97

Pudelpointer

Tail slender and straight, with stiff hair

Strongish body, short straight back

Medium-sized, hairy ears falling tight to the sides of the head

Round feet, toes close together, hard pads

Shaggy, rough, mid-length coat

A spirited dog which adores pursuing partridge, hare, and fox ... and is also an excellent retriever.

Hunting skills

The German Baron von Seydlitz created this breed at the end of the nineteenth century by crossing poodles with pointing dogs. The breed is still not widespread, although this very energetic dog is at home in all kinds of country. From the poodle side these dogs have inherited their quick wits and love of water; from the pointers, their fine nose and lively temperament. The breed retrieves well and is ideally suited to hunting partridge, hare and fox.

General appearance

According to the standard of the breed, the ideal pudelpointer resembles a heavy pointing dog in build, standing 60 cm to 65 cm/24 in to 26 in at the withers. It has a rough, tousled coat, which should be chestnut or the color of dead leaves. No white or light coloring is allowed, no brindling, and no black, except for the tiniest markings. The head is of medium length and wide, with thick eyebrows and a beard. The medium-length ears are well covered with hair and folded against the jowls. The back is short and straight, the hindquarters long, muscular and reasonably sloping. The abdomen should be smooth and high at the back; the flanks are short. The slender tail should be carried horizontally and covered with hair. In Europe the tail is generally docked for hunting.

TIPS

Training
Obedient and loyal. Be firm in training, however, right from the start. Once you have shown who's the boss you will have an excellent companion: lively, affectionate and intelligent.

In town
Like its close relatives, this breed needs space and exercise. Looking after the coat is not a great chore: regular brushing is enough.

Feeding

Once it has learned to respect mealtimes, as every dog must, this breed is a normal eater and no glutton. Home prepared or commercial food, dry or canned, will do. Food should be given in the evening, so that the dog can digest it during the night and be ready for work in the morning.

The pudelpointer is a dependable dog, undaunted by bad weather.

Weimaraner

Head well proportioned

Short, fine coat

Straight tail

Deep chest

Strong, muscular legs

*The most elegant of the German gundogs, and extremely versatile.
Also a lovable companion, quiet and good-natured.*

Hunting skills

Remarkable for both nose and perseverance. A good-sized chest gives this dog staying power, and the low stride makes for an effective turn of speed at the gallop. Suited to all terrain, the Weimaraner is a skilled gundog for every type of hunting. It holds steady as a rock on point, and can also adapt to driving or coursing game. In Germany this breed is even used as a bloodhound. Nevertheless, you have to know what you are doing with this dog.

The Weimaraner is the most aristocratic of the gundog breeds and the best all-rounder, possessing most of the qualities of the German and Central European gundogs. Its popularity grows as the years go by.

General appearance

This is a large dog: the male stands 59 cm to 70 cm/23 in to 28 in at the withers, the female 57 cm to 65 cm/22 in to 26 in. Typically silver-gray, brownish gray or mouse gray, there are short and longhaired varieties. The eyes are amber-colored, and the head clean and not too wide, in proportion to the dog's size. The muzzle is long and strong, the stop minimal and the nose dark flesh-colored. The ears are broad and long. The neck is bowed, with no dewlap. The front and hind legs are parallel, and the chest is deep.

TIPS

Training
This submissive, docile and steady dog is good-natured and easy to train. Its innate perseverance means that it can handle any terrain, but thorough training is also needed.

In town
Needs regular long walks to compensate for apartment living, but this breed makes a good pet. Quiet, adores children, and is tolerant of other animals.

Feeding

The Weimaraner doesn't need a great deal of food, though more of course in the hunting season. Meals should be balanced, or both health and performance may be adversely affected.

Pointer

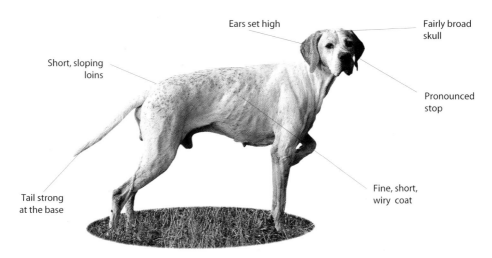

Ears set high

Fairly broad skull

Short, sloping loins

Pronounced stop

Tail strong at the base

Fine, short, wiry coat

This gundog is a specialist in open country, and can be trained to retrieve. Easy to keep, easy to train, and a boisterous companion.

TIPS

Training
Needs gentle training without stress. Keep your self-control if you want your dog to do the same. To the puppy, everything in reach will seem to call for pointing – but the difference is soon learned, and you don't have to ram the lesson home.

In town
Good-natured and quiet. Some are more demonstrative and make splendid town dogs, but need wide open spaces for a good run.

Hunting skills

The pointer is a great finder of game, and can work in extreme conditions. Remains rock steady at the point while its handler comes up. This breed is a specialist in open country, but also makes an outstanding hunter of woodcock and a useful asset in the woods. An ideal dog for grouse, hare and rabbit on high ground. Can be trained to retrieve and works well in this role on land and in the water.

General appearance

The pointer is powerfully built and, like all the British gundogs, bred for sustained running.

The pointer is often described as a 'thoroughbred,' and deservedly so, with its fine silhouette, charm and energetic sparkle.

The chest is deep and the hind legs long and muscular, with long, straight hocks for a full-powered gallop. The front legs are also straight and powerful, with well-set feet that can withstand a long day's hunting. The pointer has an intelligent expression, with its long head, well-marked stop, and gold or deep brown eyes. The coat may be any of a number of colors, usually on a white background. Height 55 cm to 65 cm/22 in to 26 in.

Feeding

Any kind of food, whether commercial or home prepared, suits this dog, provided it's of good quality: a pointer's energy requirements are high. Avoid fat, or your dog will put on weight, especially when not active every day. But this breed must be well fed from the start to avoid defects such as deformities of the limbs, which affect running ability. Reckon on 450 g/16 oz a day of a dry whole food out of season, and 700 g/25 oz for a hunting dog.

English setter

Elongated head

Long silky coat, slightly wavy

Low-slung ears

Strong, muscular legs

Tail with wide fringing

A true artist with unmistakable style, this is one of the genuinely great breeds.

TIPS

Training
Take it one step at a time, and be very gentle with this dog. It pays to be observant. This breed loves hunting and is eager – sometimes too eager – to please, but is not a difficult dog to train.

In town
Hunting is the English setter's first love, but it will adapt well to town life and can be gentle, even cuddly, so long as its hunter's instincts are satisfied. A garden is a must.

Hunting skills

This breed has the great advantage of being suited to any terrain: woodland, open country, or marshy ground. Its long coat gives valuable protection from bramble scratches. As quick thinking as a pointer, as good a stayer and just as fast over the ground, the English setter quarters rapidly, but finds the game thanks to its very acute sense of smell. Woodcock hunters love this dog, a specialist in wild small game species, which can also be trained to retrieve.

General appearance

This is an elegant dog, slight and slender, with a deep chest. The head is characteristic: elongated,

with a pronounced stop and a long, straight muzzle. The oval skull has a bump on the occiput. The ears are set low and well back; the hazel eyes are bright and brimming with intelligence. The dog has a muscular neck and varies in height from 55 cm to 65 cm/22 in to 26 in. The preferred color is white, with black patches for the blue belton, tan or lemon for the lemon belton, and liver-chestnut for the liver belton: there are also tricolor versions.

Feeding

The English setter is neither large nor greedy. When not working, it needs only 450 g/16 oz of a dry whole food a day. Hunting requirements, though, are much greater: around 700 g/25 oz a day, to replace all the energy used in the pursuit.

This efficient and elegant British breed is becoming ever more popular.

Gordon setter

Flat coat without kinks

Well-developed skull

Straight or slightly up-curved tail

Good deep chest, not too wide

This gundog has been bred for its skill on difficult terrain, and can also be trained to fetch. An affectionate living companion.

Rustic but stylish, the Gordon setter is the perfect dog for the hardships of really wild country.

length, with muscular hind limbs. The female Gordon stands around 62 cm/25 in and the male around 66 cm/26 in. The coat is a uniform glossy black with not a trace of rust, but with flame marks of bright chestnut red.

Feeding

This dog is so active that only good quality food will do, whether made at home or bought in. During the hunting season you should reckon on 700 g/25 oz a day of a dry whole food. At other times, around 450 g/16 oz is enough.

Avoid fat or anything else that could be fattening outside the hunting season. Setters are fairly lean dogs, and they should not be allowed to get plump.

Hunting skills

Bigger and stronger than the English and Irish setters, the Gordon can cope with the hardest and most testing terrain, including mountainous country. Although good after any game, this dog really excels at hunting woodcock. It is just as skilled at retrieving, and doesn't hesitate to go in after a bird that happens to fall into water.

General appearance

This is one of the most stylish gundogs, and its intelligence and dignity are tremendously engaging. The bright, intelligent eyes are full of tenderness. The stop is clearly marked, the cheeks less so, while the muzzle is long and the ears slender. The body is of medium

TIPS

Training
Setting comes naturally, and the trainer's job is to refine this instinct – not a hard job, as this setter is an apt pupil. Its natural obedience makes for a rewarding pet. Enjoys playing with children and is popular with them.

In town
Running free and hunting are what this dog likes best. Living in town, you must provide opportunities for letting off steam.

Irish setter

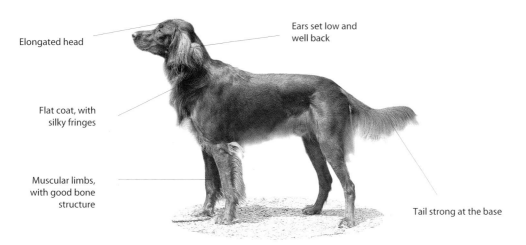

Elongated head

Ears set low and well back

Flat coat, with silky fringes

Muscular limbs, with good bone structure

Tail strong at the base

The Irish setter is an excellent hunting dog, a real enthusiast.
Affectionate and irresistible.

Hunting skills

The Irish setter is especially suited to the wildfowl that visits the wetlands of Ireland. That is where the breed began, and it never shirks the water. But it hunts other types of game just as well, in woods or open country. All setters have speed and stamina, the Irish not least, but once into thick undergrowth they take care not to leave the hunter behind. This is not an easy dog to work with, and not the dog for a novice. But it's a keen hunter with great persistence on the trail of game.

TIPS

Training
This is the most highly strung of the setters, and you must use a little psychological subtlety to bring out the best in this fairly determined character.

In town
The Irish setter makes a fine apartment-dweller provided it gets plenty of exercise. It really needs a garden. Gets on well with other animals and makes friends with children.

General appearance

This dog looks all fire and flame, and is by general agreement one of the most handsome gundogs. The mahogany coat and elegance of line are the essence of these good looks. It has a fine head, long and clean, with a pronounced stop. The eyes are nut-brown or darker, and the delicate mid-length ears are set low. The chest is deep, the forelegs straight and muscular, the hind legs long. The longish coat has splendid feathering on the legs and tail. Height 55 cm to 70 cm/22 in to 28 in, weight 20 kg to 30 kg/45 lb to 65 lb.

Feeding

These dogs are not ruinous to keep: they are moderate feeders and will eat almost anything, commercial brands or home prepared food. Normal rations are around 450 g/16 oz of a dry whole food a day, increasing to 700 g/25 oz when working.

Speed and persistent questing are the hallmarks of the Irish setter, making for an effective hunter.

Rhodesian ridgeback

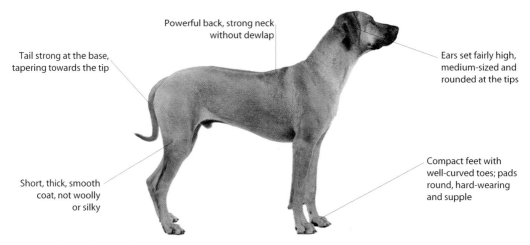

Powerful back, strong neck without dewlap

Tail strong at the base, tapering towards the tip

Ears set fairly high, medium-sized and rounded at the tips

Short, thick, smooth coat, not woolly or silky

Compact feet with well-curved toes; pads round, hard-wearing and supple

This African breed has a ridge along its back, a feature which has made it the most frequently photographed dog of all.

Hunting skills

Before the Dutch settlers arrived in South Africa, there was already a local breed of dog with a dorsal ridge of hair growing in the opposite direction to the rest of the coat. From the seventeenth century onwards, the Boers crossed these with their own dogs. The breed's native hunting grounds, formerly part of Rhodesia, are today in Zambia and Zimbabwe. Over the years, various crosses have transformed this hunter of lions into a guard dog and pet. It's widely kept in the USA, the UK, Germany and the Netherlands.

Although not much used for hunting nowadays, this breed is prized as a guard dog and companion.

General appearance

This dog has a pleasing silhouette, with a flat skull, broad between the ears. There should be no wrinkles in the skin when at rest. The famous ridge sports two swirls of hair behind the shoulders: its shape is reminiscent of a broad sword (up to 5 cm/2 in across), tapering gradually to a point at the rump. The coat varies in color from wheaten to tawny red. Head, trunk, legs and tail must all be the same color, but a little white on the chest and toes is allowed.

TIPS

Training
This dog can be quite unfriendly and guarded toward strangers. It has a strong sense of territory, but is even-tempered and confident. Loyal but not clinging, with a reputation as a bit of a character. Firm training is therefore needed.

In town
Needs a great deal of exercise, so town life is not recommended. The short thick coat needs no special attention and is good for keeping out the weather.

Feeding

Some individuals weigh more than the standard for the breed (30 kg to 40 kg/66 lb to 88 lb), and rations must be adjusted to the dog's size.
Food can be given as two meals a day, the larger in the evening. Dry biscuit and canned dogfood are properly balanced and easy to digest; they are perfectly suitable, and easier to serve than home prepared food.

Pont-Audemer spaniel

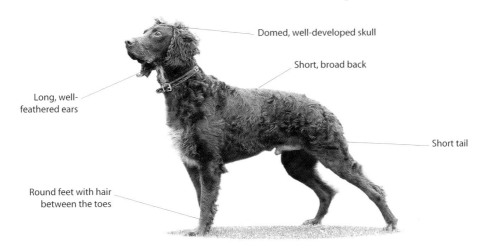

Domed, well-developed skull

Short, broad back

Long, well-feathered ears

Short tail

Round feet with hair between the toes

This gundog is also excellent in the water, and lovable in both appearance and character.

Hunting skills

A prince among spaniels. Originating from a cross between the Picardy spaniel and waterfowl hunters (the water spaniel and Irish water spaniel), the Pont-Audemer spaniel is first and foremost a water breed. Cold and wet mean nothing to this dog, which will boldly dive in without a moment's hesitation. Tremendously energetic and hardy, it is full of curiosity and driven on by love of the chase. Also quite a steady pointer, good in cover as on any terrain. An accomplished retriever, splendid at working snipe.

This dog excels on riverbanks and marshy ground. The thick, slightly oily coat is effective in keeping out the cold and wet.

General appearance

This vigorous breed is of medium height (standing between 50 cm and 60 cm/20 in and 24 in) and quite squat. The rounded skull sports a tuft which overlaps the ears, and the head is slightly pointed. The ears are set low and feathered. The hair on the cheeks is smooth, while the rest of the body is covered in thick curls. The neck is clear of dewlap, the back quite short and the flanks high. The tail is short and straight. The coat may be chestnut colored, or chestnut with gray highlights.

TIPS

Training
Easily handled, patient and gentle. This breed suits just about any hunter, and responds well to considerate treatment.

In town
Nothing less than a house with a garden will do for this rustic breed. Given that, it adapts extremely well to life in town, and this affectionate dog has infinite patience with children.

Feeding

A moderate eater: reckon on 400 g/14 oz of meat a day in home prepared food. Commercial dogfood, dry or canned, is also suitable. This is a rustic breed of born hunters, with sparing appetites.

Hungarian Vizsla

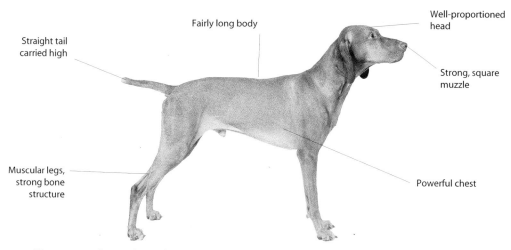

Fairly long body

Well-proportioned head

Straight tail carried high

Strong, square muzzle

Muscular legs, strong bone structure

Powerful chest

Easy to train and good at all sorts of tasks, this is a good hunting partner and an excellent companion in the home.

Hunting skills

Shorthaired or wirehaired, this breed suits every situation. The wirehaired variety, with a coat 3 to 4 cm/1 to 1fi in long and a thick undercoat, is better adapted to the cold, to difficult terrain and to working in water. Like all Central European dogs, this is an all-round hunter, ideal for the versatile hunter who goes after different game according to the season.

General appearance

The Vizsla is attractive on many counts, a good-looking as well as a hardworking dog. It is well proportioned, with a glossy, sandy-colored coat and eyes to match. (Avoid pale-eyed individuals.) It has a prominent occiput and a straight nose set in line with the fore-head. The muzzle is strong and square. The mid-length ears are fairly broad, with rounded tips, and fall flat against the cheeks. The tail is set on quite low. Stands between 50 cm and 65 cm/20 in and 26 in at the withers.

TIPS

Training
A dog with many good qualities: obedient, friendly, eager to please, and highly intelligent. No problem to train and a quick learner if handled gently. As a natural retriever, it soon learns to bring in game.

In town
This affectionate dog makes a good pet. Loves a good run and needs frequent exercise.

Feeding

Except in the hunting season, when rations should be doubled, the Vizsla doesn't need a lot of food. For normal rations, reckon on about 400 g/14 oz of meat daily. Commercial dogfood is just as suitable as home prepared food, being formulated to meet all the dog's needs at any age.

In the field, the Hungarian Vizsla is biddable and sensitive. Quarters the ground in the time-honored European way, holds still on point and is a keen, instinctive retriever.

Golden retriever

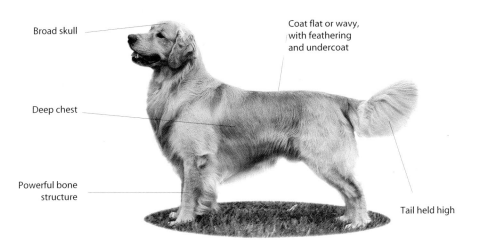

Broad skull

Coat flat or wavy, with feathering and undercoat

Deep chest

Powerful bone structure

Tail held high

Excellent on marshy ground or even in cover. Cuddly as a teddy bear, and a great retriever in the field, this is also a gentle and sensitive companion.

Just as effective as the labrador, the golden retriever is intelligent but calm.

Hunting skills

This breed has skills similar to those of the labrador. Golden retrievers love the water, too, enabling them to locate game in the most difficult conditions. Rain, wind and snow cannot prevent this sturdy and powerful rustic dog excelling in all sorts of country, from marshy ground to thick scrub. With its superb memory, this dog can retrieve game in the order it was seen to fall, and it can also be trained to quest, though this is not its specialty.

TIPS

Training
The golden retriever is reputed to be even quieter and more sensitive than the labrador, so training must be done with some finesse. Your dog will learn quickly if you don't harry it and give plenty of rewards. This is a loving and obedient dog that soon grasps what is expected of it.

In town
Adapts easily to town life, so long as it gets plenty of company and attention. Like all retrievers, needs long walks to unwind, and gets on better if there is a garden. But this steady and patient dog can be very gentle.

General appearance

The golden retriever is physically similar to the labrador, but with a longer body and a rounder head – and, of course, that familiar wavy, feathered coat. The body is robust and well proportioned, with a good deep chest and strong, muscular hind legs. The coat can be any shade of gold or cream; a few white hairs are allowed on the chest only, but no patches. Height ranges from 50 cm to 60 cm/ 20 in to 24 in.

Feeding

The golden retriever needs around 400 g/ 14 oz of red meat a day, or 500 g/18 oz of a dry whole food. Commercial dogfood, carefully formulated to meet the dog's needs, is perhaps even to be preferred. That way you avoid malnutrition, which could affect health and performance, as well as excess, which could lead to obesity.

Flat-coated retriever

Long head, flat skull

Flat, thick coat with feathering

Small ears

Deep, broad chest

Muscular legs, good bone structure

This very elegant retriever is at its best on marshy ground. Docile, friendly and loyal, it also makes an excellent family pet.

TIPS

Training
Steady but full of energy, this dog wants to cooperate, and will learn from sheer eagerness to please. It has intelligence and a good memory on its side, but there is also a slightly unpredictable, playful streak that calls for a little subtlety in training.

In town
Like all retrievers, lives happily in the home, but on account of an excitable tendency needs very frequent exercise.

Hunting skills

This is the fastest-moving of the retrievers when questing. It is also the most highly strung of the group. The flat-coated retriever can perform amazing feats, such as bringing back game that has fallen into the middle of a fast-flowing river. Their numbers are gradually growing, but this breed still deserves to be better known among hunters.

General appearance

The first thing you notice about this dog is its lively and intelligent expression. It is good-natured and cheerful, and powerfully built without being heavy. The chest is deep and quite wide, the hindquarters muscular and the feet round and strong. The head is long with a flat skull, not too broad, and the nose is a good length, with well-opened nostrils. The small ears are held close against the head. The thick, glossy coat, fringed at the legs and tail, is black or liver. The eyes are a dark chestnut. Height 56 cm to 61 cm/22 in to 24 in.

Feeding

This rustic breed isn't fussy. It has some body fat, to withstand freezing water, but weight shouldn't exceed 30 kg/65 lb. Reckon on 500 g/18 oz a day of dry food, or 400 g/14 oz of red meat, and more when working. A balanced diet is important for the sake of health and performance.

The flat-coated retriever is at home in open country and woodland, as well as in the water.

Labrador

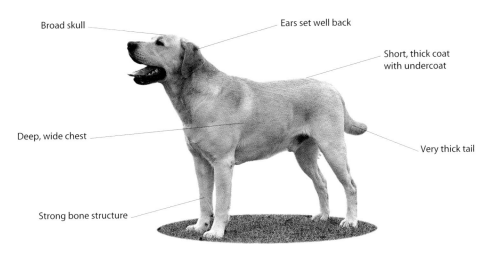

Broad skull

Ears set well back

Short, thick coat with undercoat

Deep, wide chest

Very thick tail

Strong bone structure

The most widely kept of the retrievers, with a better sense of smell than most. The labrador is a good sport, and makes an ideal hunting partner.

Hunting skills

This most imperturbable of dogs refuses to be distracted from the job in hand. A labrador will mark the fall of a bird, find the spot, and retrieve – and if two birds were seen to fall, it will bring them back in order. This is the ideal dog for driving before guns, and a favorite among wildfowlers too. It will stay for hours by the hunter's side, and then at a word will brave the morning dew or plunge into cold water to fetch the fallen duck.

General appearance

The labrador is a muscular, powerfully built dog. It has a broad head and chest, signaling strength. The breed's characteristic expression

The tough but elegant labrador has become the most famous retriever of them all.

is one of intelligence and friendliness. The coat, too, is unique: short, thick and slightly wiry to the touch, with a waterproof woolly undercoat. The coat is a solid color: it may be black, liver, or yellow, but it mustn't have any patches. The male labrador stands between 50 cm and 60 cm/20 in and 24 in tall.

Feeding

It's generally reckoned that one labrador in three is overweight. To avoid your dog getting fat, you need to be quick to work out what rations it needs.

These are rustic dogs, and in general they need no more than 400 g/14 oz of red meat a day.

TIPS

Training
The labrador is probably one of the easiest hunting dogs to train: quick to learn, with an excellent memory for everything it is taught. This means that you need to be on your guard and make sure that things go right: bad habits can be picked up as easily as good.

In town
Adaptability is this breed's hallmark: the labrador loves to hunt and enjoys the wild, but loves its owner and its owner's family best. So this dog can be happy in town, but it will pine and be miserable if left alone all day.

Bavarian mountain scenthound

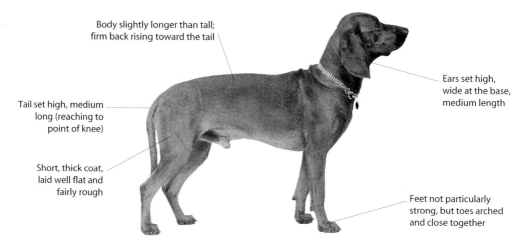

Body slightly longer than tall; firm back rising toward the tail

Ears set high, wide at the base, medium length

Tail set high, medium long (reaching to point of knee)

Short, thick coat, laid well flat and fairly rough

Feet not particularly strong, but toes arched and close together

Swift, hardy and agile, an all-terrain dog with a fine nose and a strong hunting instinct.

Hunting skills

This is the product of breeding from ancient hunting dogs chosen for their skill as bloodhounds, and from crosses between the old Bavarian and the Tyrolean hound. A breed club was formed in 1912. It's a swift runner, hardy and agile, and revels in difficult country. It has a fine nose and a powerful hunting instinct.

General appearance

Of medium height (standing 47 cm to 52 cm/ 19 in to 21 in) and fairly light build, this breed nevertheless has a muscular appearance. The body is a little elongated, with somewhat curved hindquarters and legs not too long. The chest is deep, with a long, fairly broad ribcage well let down, and the abdomen

The Bavarian mountain scenthound inherits its excellent sense of smell from the bloodhounds in its ancestry.

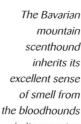

is somewhat retracted. The head is long and powerful, the skull fairly wide and only slightly arched. The heavy ears are rounded at the tips and hang close to the head. The coat is quite rough, with finer hair on the head and ears but longer and coarser on the abdomen, legs and tail. Its color may be deep red or tawny, yellow, ochre, or reddish-gray like the winter pelt of roe deer. It can also be brindle, or there may be black hairs interspersed with the background color. In red dogs, the back is brighter than the rest of the coat. The muzzle, ears, back and tail often have black hairs mingled with the rest.

TIPS

Training
A quiet and obedient dog, not easily upset and very loyal to its owner. Training presents no particular problems.

In town
This hound is more at home in the country than in town, needing like many dogs to have space and exercise. The coat doesn't need any special attention, just a regular brushing down.

Feeding

As with all hunting dogs, it's better to give only one meal a day, in the evening. This leaves all night for digestion, and the dog will be ready for anything in the morning. This breed is not difficult to keep, though you must be careful to give more food when the dog is working hard, to replace the energy used.

West Siberian laika

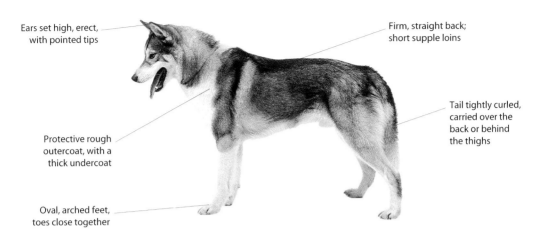

Ears set high, erect, with pointed tips

Firm, straight back; short supple loins

Tail tightly curled, carried over the back or behind the thighs

Protective rough outercoat, with a thick undercoat

Oval, arched feet, toes close together

A good all-round hunting partner, as well as a draft animal for pulling sleighs and other vehicles.

Hunting skills

This breed is the product of crossing two closely related strains of laika (laika chanteiska and laika mansiaka) with the dogs used by hunters in the northern Urals and Western Siberia. These dogs belong to the spitz family, a group with three varieties: the Russo-European laika, the West Siberian laika and the East Siberian laika. In its native region, hunting is an essential activity. Now the breed has spread widely throughout Central Russia, where laikas are raised in major breeding centers.

TIPS

Training
A steady but lively dog and very attached to its owner, even possessive. Tends to be distrustful of strangers. Firmness is needed in training.

In town
The name means 'barker.' Not recommended for apartment living: this dog needs space and a great deal of exercise. The coat is kept fine and healthy by regular brushing.

General appearance

The laika is a lively, alert dog, capable of many hunting tasks, and a draft animal into the bargain. It is of medium build, with clean lines and a robust constitution. This is a strong, muscular dog, with a well-developed bone structure, but without any heaviness or thickness. The skull is shaped more or less like an isosceles triangle, and the muzzle is long and thin, with dry chops that fit tightly together. The skin is thick, without folds, and the dense, well-developed undercoat makes the hairs of the ample outercoat stand up a little. In color the coat is white, pepper-and-salt, red or gray, with all shades between. Black is also allowed, as are dogs with contrasting tufts or streaks in the permitted colors.

Feeding

Provided the diet is well balanced, any kind of food is suitable, for these dogs are not fussy or greedy eaters. One meal a day will do. Rations should be increased in the hunting season, when your dog is working harder.

A laika bitch became the first living creature in space when she went into orbit aboard Sputnik II on 3 November 1957.

Glossary

Affix: part of a dog's registered name which indicates its breeder. Most breeders have a Kennel Club affix.

At bay: Said of a quarry that turns to face its attackers.

Back tracking: When a dog follows a trail in reverse.

Bloodhound: A dog that specializes in tracking large game that is wounded.

Bring to bay: To take a quarry by exhaustion after a long pursuit.

Cobby: Short and compact in body.

Coursing: The pursuit of running game by sight rather than scent.

Creeping: When a dog follows the scent of game at a slow pace.

Crossbreed: A dog bred from parents of different but pure breeds.

Cry: The sound made by a hound when on the trail of game.

Decoy: Prey which replaces another quarry under attack. A hound takes the decoy when it follows the new prey, and keeps the decoy when it persists after the original one.

Dewlap: A fold of skin some dogs have at the neck.

Dumbbell: An object, often made of wood, used in training a dog to retrieve.

Eager: A dog that quests actively.

Feathered: Of tail, legs or ears: fringed with long hair.

Field trial: A working trial for hunting dogs.

Figure of eight: The pattern traced by a hunting dog when quartering.

Flush: To make game fly up or run from cover.

Foiling: Losing the trail.

Give voice, give tongue: Of hounds, to cry when on the scent.

Gundog: A dog trained to follow sportsmen using guns.

Halfbreed: A dog with one purebred parent.

Hound: A dog that follows the trail of game and gives tongue on it.

Keenness: A hound's aptitude for seeking the trail beyond a check.

Mass together: Of hounds, to keep well in with the pack during the pursuit.

Muzzle: The part of the dog's head between the eyes and the nose.

Nose: Everything related to a dog's scenting ability.

Overshot bite: A short lower jaw in which the lower incisors do not touch the inner surfaces of the upper incisors.

Pedigree: A record of the ancestry of a purebred dog.

Point: A dog goes on point, or points, when it stands rigid on seeing or scenting game.

Pointer: A dog of a breed that on seeing or scenting game stands rigid looking toward it.

Purebred: A dog bred from parents of a single recognized breed.

Pursuit: The action of hounds in following the quarry.

Quartering: A systematic method of covering the ground in questing for game.

Questing: The action of searching for a trail or a quarry.

Recover the trail: To pick up the scent again after losing it briefly.

Retrace: To follow the cold trail of a quarry in order to flush it out.

Retrieve: Natural or trained behavior whereby a dog seeks and fetches fallen game.

Retriever: A dog specialized in retrieving game.

Rustic: A robust breed that adapts to difficult conditions.

Scent: The trail of smell left by game.

Scent discrimination: The ability of a dog to distinguish and follow only the scent of the desired quarry.

Scenthound: A dog that follows the trail print by print, without lifting its nose from the scent.

Stance: The set and angulation of the limbs.

Start: To make a quarry leave shelter, and pursue it.

Stop: The indentation between a dog's forehead and its muzzle.

Terrier: A breed of small dog used for turning out foxes etc. from their earths.

Tracker: A dog skilled in tracking, i.e. following the scent trail of game.

Trail: All traces of its smell that indicate the path taken by an animal.

Undershot bite: Where the incisors of the lower jaw project beyond those of the upper.

Unleash: To release pack hounds in pursuit of the quarry.

Voice: The quality of a hound's cry.

Waterfowl: The larger kinds of swimming birds that are regarded as game.

Index

Bold figures refer to the page where a detailed description of the breed is given. Figures in *italics* refer to photograph captions.

Photography credits